Confessions of a Brazilian Bikini Waxer

Dear Barbara,

Thank you so much for the the "light" and for the fun!

Love,
Remy

http://www.waxconfessions.com

Cover design: Luke Design Associates – www.lukedesignassociates.com
Inside art: Julie Goonan – www.juliegoonanillustration.com
Back Cover photo: Terry Walton – wwwebpix@aol.com
Book design: Júlio C. Dantas

To order additional copies:
www.amazon.com *or* www.booksurge.com

Confessions of a Brazilian Bikini Waxer

Reny Ryan

2008

Dedication

This book is dedicated to all the women and men out there who, while venturing into this movement of getting their privates waxed, rediscovered themselves. To those who've improved their connections with their own bodies and, as a result, their relationships. It is for those who love their bodies enough to endure the pain of waxing and the embarrassment of getting naked in front of a complete stranger. It's dedicated to the housewives and the mothers who, for a minute, ceased thinking about everyone else and decided to try something daring and delightful for themselves. To the trailblazing men dedicated to spicing up their intimate lives. It's for the young who want to shock, the old who want to be audacious, and for all the others in between.

In short, this book is dedicated to all of my clients who crossed the threshold of my studio and, with each pull of the waxing strip, shared their stories of self, family, work, and love with me.

Let there always be laughter. And absolutely no hair.

Testimonials

Confessions of a Brazilian Bikini Waxer was inspired by nearly ten years of face-to-face sessions with clients. Below is the praise for the author and her daily work.

I love the day after my wife has seen Reny. She comes home with a sexy attitude and I can hardly wait for the right moment. We try to get away, out of town, or at least out of the house. I always plan a surprise because I never know what she is showing up with. Her Brazilian bikini wax keeps our excitement up, I love it!

Sam K., San Ramon, CA - 65 years old

I go to Reny because she is so comfortable with the female body. Even if you are uncomfortable or embarrassed, she makes you feel at ease. I used to hate the word "pussy." But out of Reny's mouth it sounds so natural! I wouldn't take my pussy to anyone but Reny.

Karen. I., Danville, CA - 33 years old

Who knew such a private and sometimes painful experience could spark a friendship that I believe will last the test of time. Reny ranks up there with the "Vagina Monologue" gals—love your vagina and be proud of it. Thanks, Reny, for loving your job and sharing your passion with me (and my husband). You are the best!

Erin M., San Ramon, CA - 36 years old

If you had asked me twenty years ago if I would ever get a Brazilian, I would have laughed at you. Now, I wonder what was wrong with me. Thank heavens for the wonderful clients who tell the great stories that give others the confidence that we, too, (middle-aged people) can dare to go bare and feel beautiful.

I love the way Reny makes me feel—well, not the hot wax or the momentary pain, but the silky smooth skin afterward. While on the table Reny constantly reassures me of my feminine side, my beautiful skin, my great eyebrows, you name it—she distracts me with her sense of humor and by the time I realize it I am ready to roll.

JCM. - Alamo, CA - 56 years old

Reny is an amazing woman with an extraordinary talent! She is meticulous, a good listener, and fun. For over ten years she's been my waxer, my therapist, and above all a friend. All of the above explains why I've been with her since she was in beauty school, and to this day I look forward to my "sessions" with her.

Jana S. - Concord, CA - 52 years old

I love seeing Reny every month. Her sense of humor is contagious and the confidence in her work gives you the feeling you are in good hands so you are able to relax. Where else do you go and put yourself in compromising positions, endure pain, and laugh the whole time? She's my monthly dose of emotional healing!

Barbara J. - Pleasant Hill, CA - 41 years old

(Testimonials continued on page 139)

Contents

Acknowledgements

Writing a book is no small task, especially for me, a mother of four who tries to do everything myself. I've always had a hard time letting go of the reins. But writing (and writing and writing) this book in my second language was only ever going to be possible with tons of help.

First and foremost I must acknowledge my clients, without whom there would be no confessions. They are the core of this project, providing me with priceless subject matter and showing me their undying devotion and support these past several years. Day after day, they showed up with their stories and their commitment. Thanks to all those who told me to "keep going"; they were the force behind me. They allowed me to trespass into their private lives and share intimate details with the world. And for that I am grateful.

It was ten years ago that I graduated from Paris Beauty College, and since then my teacher and mentor Barbara has supported me with her enormous heart and serenity. Time and time again she generously gave me her time and advice, empowering me to continue on this path.

The world of estheticians is constantly growing, and when we find kindred spirits on our professional journeys, life is enhanced dramatically. I thank my beauty school buddy and first writing partner, Kelly. She has encouraged me from across the globe in Indonesia with her constant support and energy.

My sincere thanks to my most ardent followers: Linda, Jana, Jodi, Monica, Karen, Jolene, Michelle, and Erin, among hundreds other clients. I have been blessed with their encouragement throughout the years. These fascinating women inspired me and propelled me to succeed.

I am passionate about my work, but my heart belongs to my men at home. My family has been at the center of this incredible whirlwind. Thank you to my husband Jeff for his infinite patience in dealing with the long working hours, the hot flashes, and the writing. He has heard these stories over and over again, given me crucial feedback, and loved me even after I disagreed with his editing. Thanks also to my boys: Chris (18), Jair (17) and Mitchell (14) who, due to all the brouhaha with this book, may end up in therapy some day, thereby providing me material for book number two. My eldest son Julio also had an instrumental part in the development of this book. To him, I'll be eternally grateful. Whether from India, Germany, or Chile, he has never failed to come to my rescue. His breathtaking candor has kept me afloat on this long and turbulent voyage.

I could not have gotten to the finish line without the support of three people who have contributed fundamentally to this book. First, my client-turned-editor, Tiffany. She offered me her expertise and insight at a time when I was losing hope. Her contagious excitement in taking on this project boosted my confidence and provided me with the energy I needed to keep going. Second, my old and dear friend Julie, who tirelessly listened to all my worries during our morning walks and happily took on the task of sharing her artistic talents with me in the sketches presented within. Finally, Len, whose heart of gold got me to the finish line by allowing me to see one of my dreams as a well-bounded reality.

I also want to thank my readers in advance. My sole purpose in writing this book is to make you laugh, and perhaps to enhance your life in a positive way. I hope it provides, among other things, tons of laughter, or at least brings a broad smile to your face.

It is impossible to thank everyone by name. I have been blessed by legions of people—women and men—surrendering themselves to me on my waxing table over the past ten years. They, along with so many of my professional and personal friends, and their extended contacts have played a role in making this project a reality. With my heartfelt and humble thanks to everyone who has had a hand in this book, I offer you these stories as my sincerest gratitude.

Robin Williams,
on **Inside the Actor's Studio**
with James Lipton,
answering Bernard Puivot's
questionnaire from *Apostrophe*

Lipton: What is your *least* favorite word?
Williams: Cunt. Because it is so negative.
Because it is the one word that will get me
kicked out of the house.

Lipton: What is your favorite curse word?
Williams: Well, favorite, 'cuz I'm a big fan –
pussy, 'cuz it's just ... that's the opposite of the
other word we talked about [the C-word]. It's
just, so ...warm. As a friend of mine said, "You
know, I'm a big fan. We all come from there,
and we want to get back as often as possible."
Pussy. It's just so sweet, it's just ... pussy. It
reminds you of a kitty, but it's better.

You know, it's pussy. It's gentle, it's kind…It
implies affection, but still ... you gotta work.
Big fan, big fan.

Introduction

Hello, my name is Reny and I wax poosies for a living.

I know, I know. Many are not used to that word. But in my home country of Brazil we think of it just the same as any other part of the body.

Some of you may prefer va-jay-jay, or love triangle, or some other creative moniker (see p. 12 for our conclusive list). But to me, it's a pussy. And I don't whisper it. I say it loud and proud. My clients will tell you that, after just one visit with me, they start to accept the fact that they'll be hearing this word a lot. Eventually, many of them even learn to embrace the word *pussy* and stop cringing at the sound of it.

Also, if you've ever met me in person, you know that when I say the P-word it sounds like poosie. It rhymes with juicy. So, for the sake of everyone's comfort and reading pleasure that special area will heretofore be referred to as "poosie." Say it out loud with me, right now: POOSIE! But feel free to substitute your own favorite name, if it makes you feel better.

Waxing is very common in Brazil, and became my passion at an early age when, instead of playing with dolls, I often pretended I was a "waxer." I would role-play, offering my services to my Mom's friends whenever they came for lunch or coffee.

Now, every time I go back to my home town of Rio de Janeiro and get together with my childhood friends, the conversation always ends up with stories about the various and hilarious waxing experiments we all had. We talk about our different wax concoctions, the way we used to practice on each other, and everything we learned from our mistakes. We proudly share our scars from wax that got too hot or strips that weren't pulled off fast enough.

The combination of tropical weather, sandy beaches, and gorgeous people in Brazil make waxing a delightful necessity in a culture where women feel comfortable with their bodies and their sexuality. It is a country where even the pregnant women proudly display their watermelon tummies and bottoms in tiny thong bikinis—not only to look good, but also to please their men. They work hard to maintain their figures and are not shy about it. Keep in mind, though, Brazilian women don't feel they must be anorexically skinny. A little meat on the bones is sexy.

For us, the idea of having a clean poosie with only a landing strip of hair remaining is both hygienic and sexy at the same time. And, needless to say, Brazilian men love it! Our men are passionate about women, whether they're short or tall, fat or skinny, black, brown, or white. As long as they're tanned all over and showing plenty of skin, men will follow them like bees to a flower.

And speaking of men, you'll hear some stories about them, too. I get plenty of requests from male clients wanting to have their pubic area waxed. Who would've thought that men, the most fragile creatures on the planet when it comes pain endurance, would be hopping on the bandwagon? But little by little, I see my male clientele growing steadily and requesting the "Boyzilian Bikini Wax." Perhaps it's because the lack of hair down there makes their penises look bigger! Regardless of the motives, I saw a need here in the States, and I've set out to fulfill it. As soon as I graduated from Paris

Beauty College, passed the state board exam, and started my own practice, I had a crowd of wonderful clients who follow me to this day.

But it wasn't until *Sex and the City* aired that famous episode, and *Allure* and *Cosmopolitan* published articles about the Brazilian Bikini Wax—or BBW—that everything really started to change down there. Many of my clients brought me the magazines saying "Look, Reny, they're talking about the waxing style you do on me!"

Performing the BBW can be a challenge since people come in all different shapes and sizes, as well as from different backgrounds. Take Françoise for example. This French beauty can get naked and open her legs faster than I can wash my hands—while Anna's shyness at first prevented her from opening her legs wide enough for me to work on her.

Male waxing also provides enough challenges in the waxing room where a different approach is needed to deal with the "ups" and "downs" of it all. Getting an erection during the procedure can be something normal, so the trick here is to be creative enough to "deflate" the flagpoles.

While my gay, lesbian, and crossdressers clientele are easy going, the metrosexuals are a different story.

Another subject that frequently brings laughter to the waxing room is the Landing Strip. Erica wants hers a little wider, per her husband's request. "I have a big airplane," he said, "so tell Reny I need a big landing strip!" Another regular client of mine, Lynne, says she has a "jumbo jet" at home so she needs a nice spacious runway to accommodate it. But Kyoko, a petite Japanese girl with pronounced cheekbones, long silky hair and the body of a teenager, smiles shyly as she spells out her landing strip request. "I have a single–engine, one–seat Cessna at home, so give me just a little runway." We couldn't stop laughing.

Brazilian Bikini Waxing is definitely a learning experience. From open to closed legs, male erection to Landing Strips, this is positively an amazing career. But the best part of my job is meeting and getting to know all the different people who come to me for waxing. The process is, obviously, very intimate. I quickly learn about my clients' lives and loves, their children and husbands, their jobs, fears, wishes, ambitions, and inhibitions. It can be emotional. It can be surprising. It's always fun. Stripping off genital hair often strips away barriers. I get to know people perhaps better than their friends and family. And in the process they get to know themselves better than they thought they would.

Hello, my name is Reny and I wax poosies for a living. These are the stories of some of the people I've met along the way...

DEFINING THE BBW

Due to the multitude of names the BBW has acquired through the years (which varies from state to state, from salon to salon), often times I see the need to clarify some of my clients' confusion about the different waxing options available.

The bottom line is that you can have any waxing style done. Just be verbal about it to your waxer before the procedure.

Here are some options:

HEART
Some partial waxing is done while tweezers are used to shape it. The heart's contour will look perfect in wide hipped bodies

BEYOND BRAZILIAN
Removal of all the hair in the pubic, labia, and anal area

LANDING STRIP a.k.a. The Brazilian
Only a vertical strip one inch wide of hair is left above the vaginal area. Usually hair is not removed from labia or anal area

PLAYBOY STRIP
Removal of all the hair in the labia, butt cheeks, and anal area. A very narrow (1/2") strip is left in the front

LETTERS
The entire pubic area is waxed, leaving just enough hair to shape a desired letter. Tweezers are used for this thorough and methodical procedure

before   heart   beyond

a.k.a. *Beyond Brazilian*

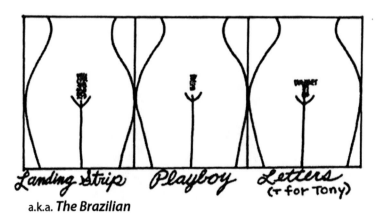

Landing Strip   Playboy   Letters
(т for Tony)

a.k.a. *The Brazilian*

My mother, aunt and friends at the beach circa 1940 in Brazil.

Girls in Ipanema Beach today

In the Beginning...

It wasn't until the mid-nineteenth century that the need for a woman's bathing suit arose. Due to the rising popularity of swimming as a sport, and a slightly freer attitude towards modesty, designers began tackling the challenge. The first swimsuits were very conservative, covering most of a woman's body. During the thirties and forties, they started to get a little smaller. These risqué bathing suits had two pieces—the top being a very large bra and the bottom a long sort of short with a miniskirt attached to it.

The reduction continued into the fifties until eventually we had the bikini as we know it today. Leaving little to the imagination and much for the delirious male libido to feed upon, this audacious, "itsy-bitsy teeny-weeny" garment became a notorious and controversial piece of women's apparel. Many countries tried to forbid the use of it, and the Catholic Church vehemently condemned it.

In Brazil, during the full regime of dictatorship, president Janio Quadros decided to ban the use of bikinis on Brazil's beaches. But, as it is with everything that is prohibited, the use of bikinis grew while their size shrank.

The bikini finally overcame its bad rap in the late sixties and early seventies with the advent of women's liberation and The Pill. Wearing a bikini became a way for women to show independence and express their freedom. The big screen also played a big role in the bikini's popularity. Actresses like Brigitte Bardot, Sophia Loren, Ursula Andress, and Raquel Welch, to name a few, owe their legacies as sex-symbols in part to this infamous garment.

But it wasn't until the seventies that a Brazilian fashion model with a perfect body and lots of attitude named Rose di Primo broke new ground with her "dental floss bikini." She soon became the object of desire for an entire nation, much to the chagrin of some and the delight of others. The "thong" would soon be adopted in many countries around the world.

A trendsetter's mecca, Ipanema Beach was the first site in Brazil where you could see a pregnant woman proudly wearing a bikini. It was the quintessential Ipanema icon, Leila Diniz, who initially had the audacity to do such a thing. She provoked a scandal across the country, but it was short-lived. Eventually, legions of expectant mothers hit the beach in their bikinis and thongs and made it fashionable. After one or two summers the taboo was broken, and Diniz was sealed as an icon. Nowadays bikinied or thonged pregnant women are a very common sight on the beaches of Brazil. And thanks to celebrities like Demi Moore, Britney Spears, and Christina Aguilera posing nude on the covers of magazines, it's slowly becoming less shocking here in the States to see a bare pregnant belly.

With the advent of the bikini and the thong came the need, of course, for the removal of more hair in the pubic area. Thus, the Brazilian Bikini Wax was born. Soon, women started waxing off more and more until eventually the only thing left on their bodies was the hair on their heads and a little Landing Strip.

As many people know, summer in Brazil is a big party. Carnival takes place in February, their hottest summer month, when the temperature can reach 110 Fahrenheit, plus humidity. Needless to say, wearing minimal clothing is tempting in weather this hot. And that's pretty much what happens: beautiful men and women worshipping the sun wearing almost nothing! The bikini tops cover only the nipples and the bottoms cover less than half of each cheek.

According to the New Edition of the *Oxford* dictionary, the definition of a Brazilian Bikini Wax is as follows:

Style of depilation in which all pubic hairs are removed, leaving only a small strip of hair in the pubic area.

Instead of the triangle of hair we all acquire during puberty, the waxer will craft a tiny strip of closely shorn hair, which we call the Landing Strip. The waxing process involves a few simple steps. First, powder is sprinkled on the area to be waxed. This helps remove moisture from the skin. Then, warm wax is applied following the growth of the hair. Finally, a muslin strip is adhered and pulled quickly in the direction against hair growth, removing the hair with its roots.

If done properly by a professional, the wax will be pulled off quickly, thereby minimizing pain. The result is a satin-soft feeling that can last a few weeks. Unlike shaving, where the hair already starts to regrow a few hours later, resulting in stubble, waxing promotes slower growth. New hair comes in finer and sparser with each waxing.

As a Brazilian, I like to think that the arrival of the BBW in the US has had its part in changing this timid culture in a positive way. I am proud when I see American women who never dared to get their legs waxed, let alone their privates, come in for their bikini transformations. It's even more astounding when I get them to spread their legs for me, a complete stranger! But we're never strangers for long.

I take pleasure in watching my clients' approaches to the waxing table whenever they are under my care. There are the ones who undress slowly, others who cover their faces with their arm, and then there are the ones who close their eyes as if to say, "Since I don't see you, Reny, you don't see me."

But they come back every month for the same ritual, uneasy or not, which tells me that it's the final product that really matters.

Trust me, the feeling of cleanliness does not go unnoticed by my clients, or whomever they share that part of their bodies with. No matter what it feels like during the procedure, they all say the same thing when they're done: "It feels great!"

La Poosita de Rosita, and Happy Husbands

Having lived in Pleasant Hill, California, for almost twenty years now, it's not surprising that I run into some of my clients now and again. I see familiar faces around town, at social gatherings, and in the gym. What's more, driving around with my license plate announcing "(heart) WAXING" makes me an easy target in this small, friendly community. But my most entertaining run-ins are with husbands of clients.

One time, as I was leaving the local YMCA, a guy asked me if I was Reny. When I said yes, he grabbed me, swung me around in an airborne hug, and said, "You are my new best friend! Thanks for the awesome job you did on my wife Abby last week."

When he put me down I was speechless. But hey, I was also happy for him, and gratified that I'd made such a difference. As we parted, he thanked me for spicing up their twenty-three-year-old marriage.

Another morning while driving to work, I was stopped at a red light on Gregory Lane when I heard someone yelling "Reny, thanks for killing the tarantula!"

Scared, I looked at the car next to me where this guy was smiling back. Just then, the light turned green and he drove away. For the longest time, I kept trying to figure out who he was and what was he talking about. It wasn't until his wife Mary came for her second waxing that I learned it was her husband who'd been the happy guy in the car that day. I then understood what killing the tarantula meant. Thinking back, yes, Mary's poosie did look a bit like that hairy creature the first time she came in!

On a warm Sunday afternoon at one of our outdoor summer concerts in downtown Pleasant Hill, my husband and I were looking for a spot on the crowded grassy area to lay down our blanket. I heard someone calling, "Here, Reny! Over here!"

I looked around and there was Steve, whose wife is a client, with a group of friends. They were offering us a place next to them. In a voice loud enough to drown out the amplified music, he introduced me to his friends saying that I was a professional waxer. The guys holding their wine looked mesmerized, and almost immediately asked me for my card. By the time I got home I realized I had never even opened my picnic basket. Those nice husbands had provided all the food and wine, and to this day their wives are regular clients.

But of all the husbands who've approached me in public, Tito is still the funniest and most memorable. I've been waxing his wife, Rosa, for the past three years, and she's a pleasure to have as a client. While I was working out at the Y one morning, Rosa and Tito came in. As she introduced me to him, she said "Honey, this is Rrrreny," with her heavy Colombian accent.

I offered my hand. He refused it and hugged me instead. He knew just who "Rrrreny" was. While we embraced, he whispered in my ear "La poosita de Rosita looks beautiful, you do excellent work!"

The Wild One

People seek bikini waxing services for a variety of reasons. Among them are personal hygiene, a feeling of freedom, and an expression of independence. And sometimes it's just about sex.

Take my client, Lorena, for example.

Lorena is vibrant and always talkative. She has no problem getting naked, jumping onto the waxing table, and spreading her legs open for me. She has this contagious energy that makes you feel like you want be her friend. She's the type you could easily go out and party with all night long.

The first time Lorena came to me, she was extremely hairy and had some trouble with the pain. More hair, more pain. I asked if she would like a shot of tequila. (I use this trick to anyone who complains about the pain on his or her first time. If nothing else, it gets them to laugh.)

She said, "No, but is anyone else in the building?" Since it was past six p.m. I told her probably not. My mistake. Upon finding out we were alone, Lorena let a loud "Oh fuuuuck, this hurts!" and she felt better.

She really makes me laugh. Or should I say, we laugh together. We share secrets, talk about our kids, and bitch about things that drive us crazy. So, needless to say, we're very comfortable together.

One day as Lorena was getting undressed before her waxing, she showed me how she dances in slow motion for her husband before they make love. She swiveled her hips to let her panties skim down to her toes, then playfully kicked them up in the air. She started gushing about how confident and sexy she's been feeling ever since she started having the BBW done—so much so that she even joined a gym and is on a diet to shed a few pounds. Turns out she's been taking a pole dancing class to learn how to strip for her husband on the weekends when the kids are with Grandma.

Oh yes, and she now also pays visits to an adult store a few times a month and is proud to say that, after almost twenty years of marriage, she finally got the courage to be audacious enough to have a "toy box" hidden in her bedroom. Unfortunately, Lorena had to find a different hiding place for her little treasure chest. Seems that her teenage daughter ran across it. She popped into the kitchen one day holding the toy box and asked "Mom, what is this?"

Without missing a beat, Lorena grabbed the box and said, "Your aunt asked me to keep this for her. I don't even know what's inside." And off she went to keep her secret stash under wraps. Now that's what I call thinking on your feet!

As it is with many of my married clients, Lorena's husband considers me a dear friend. Every time I call their house, he's always so friendly and willing to chat. You'd think we'd known each other years when, in truth, we've never even met!

Anybody who works in a career where they are affecting lives in a positive way will tell you how rewarding it is. I love seeing how people—and relationships—change after the BBW experience. I didn't consciously set out to enhance peoples' sex lives so dramatically, but it appears I have, and I am reminded of this whenever Lorena comes in. I love to hear her stories. And when she leaves me, and her pubic hair, behind, I know I am in the right profession.

Simply Lourdes

Have you ever thought that your life is running you when it should be the other way around? Life these days is beyond busy, isn't it? It seems like everybody is doing errands, picking up or dropping off kids, working, late for something...the list could go on and on. What I want to know is, why do we do this to ourselves? Why do we allow ourselves to get overburdened by the daily and sometimes unimportant chores? Trying to squeeze too many things into our already tight schedules is almost insane. Even kids nowadays are complaining about the heavy load of activities we impose on them. Our intentions are good, but are they warranted? No wonder we are becoming so dependent on stress-relieving drugs. Perhaps all we really need to do is take some time off and slow down the pace in order to have the peace we need.

Take my client Lourdes, for example. She is what many men would call a beauty with brains. She's thirty-something, has flawless dark skin, and the blackest hair I've ever seen. She's a real estate agent who talks on her cell phone about eleven hours a day, either working or chatting with clients and friends. Despite the fact that she's been a client for over two years, I really don't know much about her other than the information she wrote on her client information form that first day we met. I wax two of her girlfriends who tell me the same about her: she's always on the phone. Even during the twenty minutes she's being waxed, she schedules appointments with clients, discusses remodeling projects, schedules open houses, and closes deals. She never stops!

I cannot remember a single occasion when I have been able to carry on an actual conversation with her during an appointment. Her visits are always the same: I open the door, and she is on the phone. We hug; she walks to the room and undresses while still on the phone. She lies down and opens her legs, I apply some powder and start the procedure. I finish the job, and she's still on the phone, oblivious to what I am doing. Then she jumps up, stands before the mirror to examine the clean, tapered lines of her Brazilian, and exclaims, "Reny, I love it! You are truly an artist!"

She gets dressed while I grab the calendar so she can make her next appointment. Still on the phone, she looks at the calendar, points her manicured finger to the day she wants, and shows me the time by making signs with her fingers for one, two or three o'clock. She writes me one check to cover ten visits so she won't need to interrupt a phone call to write a check every time she comes in. We hug and I walk her to the door, where she blows me a kiss or waves good-bye, pointing to her phone apologetically.

Last winter she came in wearing a pair of those knee-high boots. While on the phone, she asked if it was okay if she did not remove them since they were hard to put back on. I said, "No problem."

During the procedure, I looked at her—naked with the boots on—and it suddenly seemed like one of those *Playboy* centerfolds. Her luscious black hair fanned out over the pillow, her dark skin contrasting so well with the white sheet, and the boots made for quite a sexy image. At one point, her call got put on hold, so I mentioned this to her and she just smiled. When the call ended she asked me to take a picture of her using her cell phone. She posed on her side with her legs in midair and sent it to her fiancé. He called immediately from work thanking her for the surprise. He couldn't talk because he also was in an important meeting but he couldn't wait to see her later. Birds of a feather, I suppose.

Despite Lourdes' busy life, once in a while she surprises me with a phone call just to say hi and to apologize for not being able to talk more during her visits. One time she even stopped by while in the neighborhood just to give me a hug. I love moments like these, because they show me that she does care about the fact that, for a few minutes each month, I am the person who takes care of her in a very intimate way, and that she appreciates it. Then, in the middle of her appreciation, her phone rings...and she's off again.

If you are like Lourdes, always on the go, take a break. Stop the marathon of life for just a moment and celebrate the good things. Enjoy some quality time with your family or a dear friend. As the old adage goes, stop to smell the roses. Or wake up and smell the coffee...I do!

Code Name POOSIE

In my years of waxing, clients have come to me with a diverse set of names they are familiar with to call the poosie. Below are some of the most imaginative ones….

Va-jay-jay (Oprah's Creation), perereca, perseguida (both Brazilian), coochie-snorcher (from The Vagina Monologues) pussy, vertical smile, beaver, cooch, cooter, punani, lovebox, poontang, love canal, flower, nana, pink taco, muff, chocha, black hole, carpet, cavern, cherry, chacha, fuzzy wuzzy, kitty kat, Jewel box, rosebud, love triangle, cupid's cupboard, mumbler (Aussie), crotch waffle, hot tamaki, beaver teeth, mumble pants (Sweden), ninja boot, Marcia (Aussie), chia hole, lip jeans, beetle hood, flap-over, furrogi (Poland), fortune nookie (China), bearded taco, hairy heaven, snake charmer, Brazilian caterpillar, mound of Venus, Venus butterfly, wolly bolly, foxhole, hot pocket, Mu'ni (Greek and pronounced like Mr. Muni of I Love Lucy), Mu'na (A "bigger" Greek), head catcher, Lawrence of A Labia, ponchita, muffin, the promised land, vegetarian's temptation, the vegan store, Amazon forest, coochie, poochika, big Montana, noochie, mystical fold, lavender, yoni (Hindi), xibiu (Brazilian Portuguese), velvet, sleipetorva (Norwegian) puke/puki (Filipino), kuku almeja (Spanish), asoko (Japanese), cha cha (South Park), chatte (French), el corte Ingles (Portuguese: "the English cut"), et cetera (old English euphemism)

Stripping Away Inhibitions

Telling anyone to drop his or her drawers and strip naked can be a delicate thing. It's daunting for most people. Add to that the knowledge that someone is about to apply hot wax to your most sensitive parts and, well, it's enough to make almost anyone a little tense.

Some folks have no inhibitions at all. And for others, getting a BBW—while intimidating at first—has a way of letting all those comparatively minor fears go. People quickly realize it's not as bad as they thought, and the results are far beyond what they ever expected.

Take Lucia, a beautiful brunette in her mid–thirties with short hair and olive skin. She was one of those women who belonged to what I lovingly call the Prude Group. They are deeply embarrassed, at least initially, and yet they'd found something inside them that gave them the strength to go ahead and try the BBW, even if it meant getting naked in front of a stranger. Lucia took her time filling out her paperwork at the beginning of our first session. When I finally told her it was fine and asked her to disrobe, she looked at me a bit wide–eyed.

"Even the underwear?" she asked.

"Yes, my darling, even the underwear," I affirmed.

Her eyes widened even further and I could tell fear was chilling her veins, but I just ignored it.

"Just hop right up here on the bed, open your legs, and

I'll explain to you what the BBW entails," I said. My secret is to keep talking so my clients don't have time to think about how embarrassed they might be about the situation.

"How is work going?" I asked, trying to distract her.

"Oh, fine, fine," she responded, somewhat breathless.

"What is it you do again?" *Keep her talking, ask questions*, I thought. Slowly she started to relax. "How is your family? Do you have a boyfriend? Where did you grow up?" I kept tapping into my arsenal of small talk. Soon, despite her initial fear, Lucia's wax was done. I gave her a small hand mirror, expecting her to take a quick glimpse, considering her shyness.

But to my surprise, Lucia jumped off the bed and stood naked in front of the full-sized mirror, turning from side to side, admiring herself at length. I was starting to think she'd forgotten I was in there when she said, "Wow, Reny, I really love my new poosie!"

Her total enthusiasm about the results surprised me— the BBW spurred quite a change from the girl who ten minutes ago didn't want to take off her underwear, much less mention the word *poosie*.

"Let's schedule my next appointment," she said eagerly.

For Lucia, one appointment changed her whole attitude. For Anna, it took a bit longer. Anna is an extremely shy girl from Sri Lanka. Some of her friends are my clients, and for quite sometime they'd been trying to convince her to come and try the BBW. I could barely hear her voice when she greeted me upon her arrival. After filling out her client information form, she undressed very slowly as if wondering what she was doing there.

Walking to the bed, Anna had the air of a condemned man on his way to the electric chair. She lay on her back with her legs about an inch apart, eyes closed, fists clenched, and one arm over her face as if she could hide from the world. I told her about the waxing process and what I was planning to do.

"I need your legs open so I can start," I said gently.

"They are open," was her faint reply.

"Well, I need you to spread them a little more so I can apply the wax."

She didn't respond. I spent a few minutes talking and trying to get her to relax, asking her again to open wider. Finally, I had to hold her legs open with one hand and apply the wax with the other. Once in a while she would resist and then all of a sudden she would relax and I'd press open her legs a little bit more and take advantage of those precious minutes to finish the job. All throughout Anna's first session I asked her if she really wanted to do this and she kept saying yes. I believe everyone, especially women, should decide what's best for them; so I trusted her word and went with it, despite the effort it was taking to keep her legs open.

To my surprise, after we'd finished, Anna asked to schedule another appointment. I looked at her, a bit quizzical.

"I'll do another appointment on one condition. You have to promise to open your legs on your own next time," I said gently, looking her in the eye to gauge her reaction. She nodded sheepishly.

During our second appointment together, Anna was much more relaxed and willing to cooperate. Now, that a few years have passed since our first meeting, Anna is a completely different person when she comes into my studio. She walks into the room, undresses, and jumps on the bed like a pro. We both had a good laugh recently when she came in to have her eyebrows waxed but before I said anything she was nude.

"Anna, I thought this appointment was for your eyebrows," I wondered out loud.

She laughed. "Force of habit, Reny, force of habit. Sorry."

What a difference time and confidence makes, I thought. At one point, Anna had told me that, other than her doctor, I was the only person she would ever open her legs for. Of course, that has changed, too. Anna got married and is a much more—shall we say, "open"—woman these days!

For God's Sake

If you saw Joanna in a lineup of women, you would never pick her out as the one who gets a BBW. You wouldn't even think she'd shave her legs. I mean, she reminds me of the nuns at my childhood Catholic school in Brazil. Her skirts are always well below the knee, her shirt is always buttoned to the throat, and she wears her hair a la Dustin Hoffman in *Tootsie*.

But Joanna is the salt of the earth. A mother of four, she is extremely active in her children's school and extracurricular activities. Religion is important. In fact, I usually get an earful about how valuable faith is and how people today have become too materialistic. While I agree she has a point, I have learned to steer clear of religion and politics.

However, never once has Joanna missed or been late for an appointment. And she drives over fifty miles to see me! Meticulously organized and efficient, this woman shows up without fail and wastes no time getting right to business. The first time I met with her, I showed her into my treatment room and before I had time to check the temperature on the wax, this lovely, conservative, God-fearing lady had stripped off those matronly clothes and plopped her naked self right up there on my table, legs spread and ready to go.

Maybe she just wants to get it over with, I thought. But the more I get to know her, the more familiar we become with each other, I know it's just that she trusts me. I like to think we have the kind of relationship most women have with their gynecologist: I'm a trusted professional and I'm providing a service. I'm sure there are many waxing providers closer to and more convenient for her. In a way, I am honored she has "chosen" me. I knew I was getting to know Joanna better when she confided in me—to my surprise, once again—that she always tries to have great sex with her husband the night before he goes on a business trip. No matter what time he has to get up in the morning, she goes the extra mile to make sure he leaves satisfied. Wouldn't want to send him away wanting, now would we?

But nothing prepared me for the time I met Father Joseph.

It was towards the end of a fairly routine appointment, and we were chatting about what the rest of the day held for us. "Oh, I'm going to take my kids and Father Joseph out for ice cream," she said.

"Father Joseph?"

"Yes, he's a dear friend. He drove me to my appointment today. He and the kids are outside, reading the Bible."

I couldn't resist. "He's here? Does he know you're here waxing your poosie?"

"No way, I'm here to 'wax my legs'" she replied.

She went on to say that Father Joseph was their adopted grandfather, of sorts. He was all alone and they had taken him under their wing. I walked Joanna out when we were through, and sure enough, there was a kindly old priest with her four children. And they were reading the Holy Bible.

After they left I thought about how important her BBW must be for Joanna to ask her priest to drive an hour away and babysit her children. I learned a new lesson that day from the old cliché: "Don't judge a book by its cover."

And from then on, I've never assumed anything again.

The Art of Being Resourceful

Being resourceful is an attitude and an art. People who have dealt with adversities often develop an innate resourcefulness as a mechanism to navigate through life. Growing up poor in Brazil I had to learn from an early age how to make something out of nothing. The word *recycling* has been part of my vocabulary ever since I can remember. I even used to build my own toys. I remember spending a full day making a slingshot from scratch. Together with my sisters, Flavia and Flair, I searched for the perfect tree branch. We cut the branch with a bread knife, shaped it, and sanded it. For the catapult we cut an old bicycle tube and attached it to the makeshift sling. The only problem we ever ran into was learning how to share our creations, but we always managed.

I bought a fancy kite for my boys one summer, and it made me think about how my sisters and I had spent hours making our own. We would walk the woods near my home for bamboo stalks that we then shaped into sticks for the frame. We'd use recycled wrapping paper for the screen. Cooked rice was our glue, along with a little of mom's sewing thread. What a great feeling it was to see our homemade masterpiece flying high in the sky—so simple, but so beautiful!

Another vivid childhood memory for me is when I learned to ride a bike. We didn't have a small one that fit me, so I had to use my father's bike. It was enormous and weighed a ton compared to my skinny six-year-old body. At the end of each day I would come home with scrapes and bruises all over my legs. But boy, was I happy! It took me almost a week to learn how to ride that big bike, but at the end I was so proud of myself. I wouldn't come in until past dark.

So, given my resourceful background, I didn't despair when, during a big winter storm, I found myself with a full appointment book and no electricity. My cell phone was out of juice and I had only a cordless phone available, so I couldn't call my clients to cancel or reschedule their appointments. Consequently, I had to find the best way to cope with the situation.

I started my day by running to the nearest hardware store, where I bought a camping stove and a propane tank. I placed all the wax rollers in a double boiler and took a deep breath. *So far, so good,* I thought. The next step was to find a way to bring natural light into the street-level waxing room without exposing my clients in their compromising positions. For that I removed the blue veil I have decorating one of the mirrors in my office and covered the window with it, allowing some daylight in but still obscuring the view from outside.

Now I would have to figure out how to keep the room heated. Unfortunately, I couldn't come up with any solutions for that short of building a bonfire. However, since many of my clients sweat during the whole waxing process, I decided that fire wouldn't be necessary. It does bring up the point, though: we've come a long way from being cavewomen, haven't we?

My final obstacle: how was I going to be able to see well enough to do my job thoroughly? I usually use a fairly bright magnifying light, the kind you see in a dentist or dermatologist office. As I was pondering this predicament, the battery-operated bell rang; my first client had arrived. It was Debra, and she was surprised to see me ready to work in an almost-dark shop. She asked the obvious question: "How are we going to do this, Reny?"

"Don't you worry," I said as I walked her to the waxing room.

Eat Your Heart Out McGyver!

She saw all the arrangements I had made and started to laugh, proclaiming, "This should be an adventurous waxing experience. Waxing in the dark!" As she lay down, I handed her the two flashlights I had grabbed on my way to answer the door. Debra held them towards her poosie, while I kept running back and forth from the camping stove with the waxing rollers. During the whole time, thankfully, we both kept our good senses of humor.

Debra reminded me that she had also been with me the summer Northern California had those rolling blackouts. She arrived just a few minutes after my number came up on the grid map and the electricity went out. Without wasting a minute, I moved the waxing rollers outside into the 110-degree summer heat. The scorching pavement below and sun blazing down from above kept the wax soft all day, allowing for perfect BBW in the height of bikini season.

But back to my stormy day. In the end, I had eight happy clients. Each and every one of them now has a story to tell about their "Commando Waxing" complete with propane tanks and flashlights. I appreciate their cooperation and spirit of resourcefulness.

As I have matured over the years with my children, I realize more and more that the secret to success in life is not to despair when faced with a difficult situation. Act imaginatively, be creative, and you will overcome any circumstance. If all you have are lemons—but no sugar—instead of lemonade, make yourself a margarita and enjoy being ingenious.

The Cheater

Too often in my occupation, I find myself seeing and hearing much more than I want to. On the one hand, I feel honored that my clients trust me as their confidante—sort of how Tony Soprano confided in Dr. Melfi. On the other hand, it sometimes puts me in awkward or compromising situations. While no one has confessed to any mob-style whackings during a waxing session (so far, anyway), the story of Ramon and Sandra (and Mariela) truly tested the limits of my professional code of ethics.

Ramon is a middle-aged mergers and acquisitions executive who has been coming to me for facials and waxing every four weeks without fail for three years. Of course, any man who gives his skin that much attention has got the credentials of a true metrosexual: straight, over-groomed, and consumed with himself. Short but well built, he resembles a Latin Tom Cruise.

Although he's not famous, he has this certain bravado about him. When he walks into a room, dressed in his dark-rinsed 7 jeans and button-down Zegna shirt, he commands attention. Although you would never guess it, Ramon has been married for five years. His wife, Sandra, is also a client of mine. A blue-eyed strawberry blonde with milky Danish skin, she is as beautiful as Ramon is handsome. She stands a bit taller than him, and her lithe, feminine frame complements her striking looks. Confident and outgoing, Sandra is a successful Silicon Valley accountant at a venture capital firm. No man ever held her interest very long, until the day friends introduced her to Ramon at an Irish pub in San Francisco. Soon they merged and became the ultimate power couple.

Sandra and Ramon have no children, partly due to their career focus. Ramon's job requires him to travel a lot, and he often tells me about his trips, complete with photographs. But there was another reason for their childlessness, as I was about to find out. While booking Ramon's appointment one day, he asked me if I wouldn't mind doing a BBW for 'his dear friend Mariela.' I scheduled her in and didn't give it another thought.

A week later, Ramon showed up with a stunning Spanish girl who had long, black hair and gorgeous dark eyes. She reminded me of many of the Brazilian girls I grew up with on the beaches of Rio. Her accent was captivating, as was her figure. Mariela was all of twenty-nine.

From the moment they arrived, I got that feeling that women get in the pit of their stomachs when they know something just isn't right. It's a feeling that makes you want to call your best girlfriend and share, but unfortunately I had no time for that. I had to play it cool, even though I knew from their body language and smiles that she was more than a "dear friend."

After introductions, Ramon was about to leave Mariela under my care, telling her to call as soon as she was done, when much to my surprise he grabbed her face and kissed her passionately. My mind started to race, and that feeling in my stomach turned to nausea. Still, I decided to play dumb.

"So, what kind of shape would you like, Mariela? The BBW Playboy strip, the Beyond BZ, a heart?" I asked. Meanwhile, I was thinking I should just go ahead shave (yes, shave!) her a capital A for adulteress!

She chose the Playboy strip, of course. To make matters worse, throughout the entire procedure she wouldn't stop talking about how great Ramon was and how excited he would be with her Playboy waxing.

"I am sure he will, sweetie," I said as she lay on the table, legs apart.

"Where did you two meet?"

"We met at a resort in Majorca, an island off of Spain," she answered. "I am a cocktail waitress, and he was at the resort on business. We hit it off right away, and before I knew it, it was like we were on vacation there together. That was about a month ago. We missed each other so much I had to visit him. He flew me out here using his miles."

My mind started racing again. *Does she know he's married? What's he thinking? I know his wife! What's going on here?* Suddenly, my female emotions kicked into high gear and I got really mad just thinking about poor Sandra sitting at work, probably gazing at a picture of Ramon on her desk. Or maybe she had come home early to fix him one of her gourmet club recipes for dinner, while here I was, primping Mariela to have fabulous sex with him later.

I thought of my ex-husband in Brazil, who had cheated on me with my best friend, and all the pain that comes with betrayal and infidelity. I felt like ripping the hot wax off Mariela's young poosie the wrong way. Perhaps they would have to wait a few days till her bruised and swollen skin recovered! At the same time I was struggling with the fact that my emotions were overcoming my professional ethics. Fortunately, I got my senses back and gave Mariela what she'd requested—but I do admit, I could've been gentler.

We were looking at her pictures from their adulterous

trip to Spain when Ramon swaggered in to pick her up. He kissed Mariela again without hesitation and told her there was a surprise for her in the car.

"Be right there, *mi amor*," he said. "I just need to write Reny a check."

"Okay, honey," she replied. "I can't wait to see what it is. I love surprises! Thanks, Reny. I hope to see you again soon."

She winked at Ramon as she left, as if they had already planned her next trip here.

With that, Ramon quickly turned to me and casually said, "Reny, I'm sure I don't have to ask you to keep this to yourself."

I was appalled, to say the least. I gave him a half smirk and said, "Hey, this is your life, not mine. Do you want to schedule another appointment?"

I knew if I didn't say that, I would say something I would regret.

"I'll call you," he said. "I'm all over the place this month." Indeed.

As I peered through my shades and watched them zoom off, I realized how naïve this girl was. Mariela had no idea what was really happening as she sat in her dream guy's black Porsche Carrera. How could a beautiful, exotic girl be so desperate for love that she fell for a married man?

A few month's passed before Ramon came for another facial. He told me that Sandra had found evidence of the affair and they had separated. With tears in his eyes, he told me about her moving out. "She is barely accepting my calls. I leave her messages, send flowers and e-mails, but so far it is not looking good."

"Ramon," I said gently. "Let me ask you something. How could you risk everything and have an affair?"

"I don't know. I am not sure. I guess I wanted the best of both worlds. Sandra is a good catch, someone you find and want to marry. But after a while, the excitement—the chase—is over. I strayed looking to fill that void. I am in therapy now, trying to figure out how I got here."

He told me that he really loves Sandra, but while alone in Spain he'd felt like a teenager when he saw beautiful Mariela dancing. He was hopeful that Sandra would forgive him and that they could put all this behind them.

I asked about Mariela. He said she was back in Spain and that they had broken up. When I asked how he liked her Playboy waxing, he said that Mariela had been very sore, that she wouldn't let him get near her until it was almost her departure time. Inside I was cackling like a witch while I thought to myself, *Good job, Reny. Mission accomplished!*

Ramon and Sandra eventually got back together. During one of his facials, Ramon told me that, at his age, he needed the security and comfort his marriage with Sandra offered. Also, he had changed jobs and wasn't traveling as much, so they are closer now, enjoying each other's company.

But as we say in Brazil, trust is like a piece of aluminum foil—once wrinkled, it will never be smooth again. Which is why Sandra made Ramon sign a legal document giving her full ownership of all their assets if he is ever caught cheating again. Smart woman. "Be careful now or you may end up homeless someday," I joked.

But things can't be too bad between them. Sandra recently came in and requested the Playboy strip. I was happy to hear that—and I did it for her very gently. I wanted to ask her whose idea that was, or if they were acting like newlyweds again, but I decided to keep my mouth shut.

To this day, Sandra has never mentioned the affair, and I respect her silence. But she did tell me that they are thinking about having a baby. For my part I was glad to see that the storm had finally passed and they were happy again.

The Power of Positive Thinking

Despite the TMI (Too Much Information) factor, I usually find that my job is very rewarding. Getting on the BBW train has been a turning point for many of my clients. Perhaps it's because it awakens in them a heightened sense of awareness about their bodies, especially their nether regions. I hear from so many people that they love admiring themselves in all their smooth glory. Suddenly, they see beyond poosies, their imperfections, their insecurity and into themselves. They say they love the feeling of being clean and unencumbered. Women say they feel more feminine; men tell me their partners find them irresistible and sexy.

Many women have started paying attention to the rest of their bodies, too, targeting other areas for improvement. It varies, but some have joined weight loss programs in order to shed a few pounds, while others hit the gym more, and a few have become yoga fans. And I can't go without mentioning a few of the more brazen who've signed up for pole-dancing classes! But the ones I'm most in awe of are those who take it one step further and decide to quit smoking for good. It got me started thinking about the power of physical—and mental—fitness.

As far as exercise goes, nobody is beyond help. We all know that physical activity is beneficial and that everyone has different reasons for doing it. My clients say they exercise for weight loss, stress release, and improvement of overall health. The nice thing is that there are so many different ways to approach exercise. I meet yogis, rock climbers, step-climbers, runners, hikers, you name it—everybody waxes.

Whatever the process, the most important factor is that these waxing adventurers are nurturing themselves while embracing a positive and productive attitude toward their husbands, children, and life in general. I have no words to describe how rewarding it is for me to hear from a client that he or she experienced a "pivotal moment' right after waxing. It's as if senses were awakened and they suddenly wanted to take better care of themselves from head to toe, inside and out.

For my client Carla her waxing experience changed her life three years ago. This young woman with shiny hair, a soft voice and a beautiful smile was nearly one hundred pounds overweight. During her visits I could notice the embarrassment as she undressed and kept apologizing for the extra skin I had to wax. From my perspective all I could offer was advice about the importance of eating healthy and exercise.

I was pleasantly surprised when in one of her appointments Carla showed up excited about having lost a few pounds and wouldn't stop talking about her new exercise routine, waiting to shed a few more so that she could go shopping for smaller size clothes. She also had a new hair cut and light make-up, which allowed the world to see a much younger Carla. She said she felt good to be in charge of her new self. Her enthusiasm was contagious and to satiate my curiosity I asked her the motive behind this amazing transformation. She said: "You know Reny, for years I've never paid too much attention to myself as a woman. I was OK with the way I looked and didn't care about other people's opinion, but as soon as I got home after the first time you waxed me, I looked at myself in the mirror and realized that my pubic area looked better than the rest of my body, my face included. That was my 'a-ha moment' and I thought it was time to do something about it, and am so happy to tell you that I won't stop here. I feel so reenergized after my walks or my workouts that I can't believe I spent years ignoring myself."

Ethan is another client who after getting his back waxed started to enjoy life much more than he ever imagined. He is a single man, who used to move from place to place, and nine years ago decided to settle down in the Bay Area. He came to me referred by another male client.

Ethan has fair skin, and you would not even know he had hair unless he took off his t-shirt. Both his back and chest are dark due to the thickness of the hair on it. Despite this, Ethan had never enjoyed any activity that required being half naked. But all that changed after a few waxing sessions. Swimming, water skating and going to the beach are now part of his summer's blast. He too got rid of few pounds and told me the other day that he just got a job promotion and he's been dating again.

I cannot deny my satisfaction whenever I hear testimonials such as Carla and Ethan's and see the positive changes in many of my clients. Just being able to witness their transformation month after month and knowing that I am to some extent the person responsible for their happiness is the greatest gift of my career.

In my own life, while I don't consider myself an exercise maniac, I must admit that I do plan my work schedule around my exercise schedule. The energy I get from playing a few games of racquetball and a half–hour of weight lifting can keep me going like the Energizer Bunny, all day long.

To me, there's so much more to exercising than simply working out in the physical sense. Exercise is a social activity. In all my years at the local YMCA, I have encountered some extraordinary people and made many friends who share my passion for staying healthy.

Like my racquetball buddy, Bob, would say, "Getting old stinks. Every body part hurts and the parts that don't hurt don't work!" But he's seventy-two years old and looks great. What's more, he has a great attitude. That's the power of positive thinking at work. It gives me a great sense of satisfaction to see that my waxing has played at least a small part in transforming the way so many people feel about their bodies and themselves.

The Cleaning Power of a Good Wax Job

During an episode of *Desperate Housewives*, Lynette's husband Tom arrives home from a business trip and promptly sends the boys outside to play. He then throws Lynette on the bed and says passionately, "I love you, honey, and I need you now."

Ai, caramba! All I could think about was how he had just come in from a long day of traveling with all that airport grime on him, very little romance, and—like a lot of men—the expectation of sex.

The next day one of my clients, Susan, came in. I asked if she'd happened to see that particular DH episode, and she immediately responded, "Yeah, did you see that part were Lynette's husband comes home from his business trip, sends the boys out to play, and expects his wife to hop in the sack with him?"

She continued, "Men just expect us to be ready to rock and roll as soon as they feel the urge. Don't they understand that we need more foreplay, some romance, and a little more stimulation than just...come on, baby, lets have sex?"

"Even worse than the expectation to rock and roll," I replied, "is that they expect us to go down on a penis that hasn't been washed since morning!"

Well, the topic really got Susan on a roll. She explained that Mark, her husband, is one of those guys who tries to squeeze in a "quickie" at odd times of the day, and she absolutely hates it. Susan herself always looks very fresh and well put together. She is a brunette in her mid-forties, with almond shaped eyes and full lips—which always flaunt a sexy red shade of lipstick. Her nails are always done and her hair never shows any signs of gray, which leads me to believe that she visits her hair-stylist regularly. She is always well dressed, wears just the right amount of expensive perfume, and does a great job applying her makeup.

One day, Susan arrived looking a bit gloomy. When I asked if everything was all right, she just shrugged and nodded feebly. After fifteen minutes of unusual silence, Susan asked, "Reny, how can I convince my husband to come see you and have his crotch waxed?"

Surprised by her question, I asked, "Why? What's up?"

I could see Susan was wondering whether telling anyone about her troubles was a good idea. Finally, she sighed and said, "Okay, if I am going to vent to someone it might as well be you.

"My husband is extremely hairy...down there," she went on, "and I think all that hair is making giving him head such an agonizing experience for me. It's foul, and all that hair tickles my nose and makes me sneeze so much that sometimes I am unable to finish! Last night Mark got a little upset and said he didn't know what was worse: not having oral sex or having me stop in the middle of it because of my sneezing.

"Oh, Reny," she proceeded, "I am not kidding, I think I sneezed nine or ten times and then had to take a break in order to blow my nose; it wasn't fun for either of us, trust me."

I could feel her pain. Since the dawn of time, we women have squeezed ourselves into tight garments, worn makeup, gone on diets, shaved, waxed and—most recently—endured the pains of plastic surgery all in the pursuit of beauty, be it for ourselves, others, or the men in our lives. And what do men do? They are ready to go after a shower, maybe some cologne, and a shave. It's not fair!

"Susan, I hate to say it, but you are not alone," I offered. "I have many clients who ask me how they can get their husbands in here. At least Mark takes a shower. Some of my clients' husbands don't even do that! How do these guys expect to have great oral sex when their penis area smells like a sweaty butt hole? Sorry, but I don't have the answer for you.

"On the other hand, my dear," I continued, "my male clientele is growing steadily. I wonder if women out there are letting their voices be heard? What if we follow the lead of the women's movement in the late sixties to construct a new wives' movement? We can have signs that say WE DEMAND CLEAN PENISES and GROOM YOUR PUBIC HAIR!"

We laughed hysterically.

In the end, to support Susan, I told her to tell Mark about a Newsweek article I'd seen about male waxing. The article mentioned that once the pubic area is hair-free, the penis looks bigger and the smell goes away. Sure enough, it worked. Okay, fine, it was probably the "bigger" part that got him here, but we'll take it. Soon after, Mark came with Susan and the three of us had a great time in the waxing room. I was talkative, as usual, trying to distract Mark from the pain. Susan worked her magic by holding his hands and reminding him it would all be worth it.

"Honey," she said, "I can't wait to spend a night with you without having to reach for the Kleenex box!" Mark was in good spirits, and by the time we finished he confessed it hadn't hurt as much as he'd thought it would. "Thanks, Reny, for the good job," he said, and gave me a hug.

The following week I received a message from a hotel in Carmel. It was Susan, telling me that the sex was so fantastic after Mark had his BBW, they had decided to get away for the weekend. Once again, I felt a great sense of fulfillment. People like Susan and Mark drive me to keep going and to excel in my profession.

And just for the record, guys: hygiene is important! A clean crotch followed by a long shower just before sex will dramatically improve your sex life.

To be fair, women can also fall into the category of hairy and smelly. After all, our pubic area is a hidden, dark place, and many times moist with urine residue left in the hair. It's a big breeding environment for bacteria, which is what causes that acidic smell. Every job has its pitfalls, and that's one of mine.

BBW Quickies

Susan's husband, Jeff, came home from work one day while she was chatting on the phone with a friend. They were talking about a local gardener named Alberto who was extremely good and not too expensive. Jeff must have been eavesdropping because when Susan said:

"Wow, that's a very good price to do the bush,"

Jeff looked puzzled and started to make big thumbs-down gestures. When Susan asked him what the problem was, he said:

"Oh no, no, no, Alberto will not be doing your bush. I think Reny does a great job and I really don't want any other man looking at you."

She couldn't help but laugh hysterically as she explained to him that the bush she was talking about was the one in the garden, not hers.

**...and the Oscar for the best smelling poosie
goes to...Anne S.**
Our deepest thanks to Crabtree & Evelyn
for the creation of the Spring Rain body lotion.

Scent of a Woman

Scent was clearly an issue for my twenty-five-year-old client Sylvana. Professionally, she is a top-notch personal trainer. Her well-sculpted body is her business card and, needless to say, she is a busy girl at work. Sylvana is also a carrot top, and in the waxing room red and gray hairs are the coarsest, so waxing them is a little more challenging.

Before I go any further, let me say that little scares me in this profession. I am used to the sight of the hairy, the very hairy, and the forest hairy poosies. The truth is that I am basically immune to their smell. Part of my immunity comes from the fact that I concentrate on the area to be waxed, forgetting all else.

Well, Sylvana tested my power to focus. As she undressed, I saw the mass of red hair between her legs and thought, *Uh-oh. Her poosie hair is so long that I could easily have made an Irish Barbie doll wig with it.* And then it happened. As soon as she took her underwear off and lay on the bed I was taken aback. For a second, I felt like I was in a slow-motion scene in a movie, screaming "Nooooooooo!" while flinging myself across the room.

The strong smell inundated my small studio, killing even the aroma of the candles. I tried to not be too obvious with my reaction. Making my clients feel comfortable is very important to me.

Realizing that this was probably a challenge beyond the waxing room, I suggested I trim the hair in the main part of her poosie before I start to wax the bikini line. But Sylvana stopped me saying, "Oh no, Reny, please, I like it the way it is...looong."

"It's your choice," I replied. "But with the bikini line waxed, the whole thing will look much better if the rest of the hair is trimmed."

She said, "Oh, no, I just can't imagine short hair down there. I like the butt cheeks and the bikini area clean, but please don't trim the middle."

That said, I put the trimmer away with a sigh and started on her bikini wax.

Sylvana went on telling me about her day at work, unaffected by the stench coming from her very hairy poosie. (*Ah, yes*, I thought, *she's in Spandex all day!*) I tried to guess whether or not she noticed the smell as much as I did or if it didn't matter to her because she was so used to it. After she left, I had to open the window and the door and spray some air freshener in the room so my next client wouldn't faint from the smell.

When Sylvana returned for her next appointment, she was feeling quite happy and said, "Reny, my fiancé Ryan loved my waxed job, but last week when we went food shopping he suggested I get some personal deodorant. I don't understand."

Bingo! Now I had a good reason to convince her to trim her red bush.

"Oh, Sylvana, I'm so glad he liked you all clean down there! But, look, sometimes with our busy days of commuting, walking or sitting—trips to the bathroom included—even if we shower that morning, the pubic area can become infested with bacteria, which makes it smell bad. That's why I was urging you to trim all that extra hair. I am sure you've noticed a big improvement as far as the odor goes, no?"

She looked at me puzzled and finally said, "Go ahead, do the Brazilian and trim the hair in the Landing Strip. I just hope you're right, because I like my poosie the way it is; but hair is hair, and if I don't like it all I have to do is to wait for it to grow back, right?"

That said, I went to work and felt confident that she was going to love her new look. When she jumped off the bed and looked at herself in the mirror she said, "*Wow*, it does look good!"

Another Mission Accomplished, I thought to myself. Nowadays, whenever Sylvana comes for her appointments, she makes sure I trim her pubic hair, too.

A few months later, Sylvana came in and told me that Ryan was taking her away for the weekend and had bought her some sexy lingerie from Victoria's Secret that she couldn't wait to wear.

"Hey, girl," I said, "see what a difference a clean pubic area makes? You went from getting personal deodorants to getting sexy lingerie."

And I no longer have to air out my office.

TOP TEN
Reasons Why Women & Men Get BBW

10. No razor burn.

9. Peace of mind while on vacation.

8. The fabulous feeling of being clean, sexy, and uninhibited.

7. More skin on skin during sex— fabulous!

6. It turns guys & girls on big-time.

5. You feel young as a twelve-year-old but naughty as a pinup girl or Playgirl hunk.

4. It is so fun having a "your" little secret.

3. You look better naked.

2. It makes oral sex so much nicer for your partner.

1. If you like sun and sex, the BBW is— a must!

It's for Everyone

So, are you wondering what all the fuss is about? Almost everybody is willing to try waxing to find out how good it looks and feels (when you're finished, that is). I can't promise it will feel good while you're having it done, but I'll do my best!

Everybody has unwanted hair somewhere. And we all have our own unique reasons for waxing. Some people do it to please others, while others do it to please themselves.

Thanks to my location in beautiful Northern California, just forty-five minutes from San Francisco, I have a wonderfully diverse and eclectic clientele. They come from all walks of life. I see straight men, housewives, teenagers, bankers, teachers, actors, football players, gay men, and lesbians, to name a few. With so much focus on peoples' differences, with all the discrimination and injustice in the world, I am happy to have my own business where I welcome the infinite possibilities of types of people into my office. After all, waxing doesn't discriminate.

Well, maybe a little—against hair, that is.

But let's talk about the gay community for a moment. Ladies first. My lesbian clients are a joy to have. These women really do stick together, just like peanut butter on jelly. They schedule appointments for their partners, they buy each other gift certificates, and they bring friends along so they can see for themselves. Usually lesbian women come with their partners—not only so they can spend more time together and chat, but also to give each other some moral support.

I remember when one lovely couple, Anne and Laura, came for their appointment. Anne chose to go first, while Laura sat comfortably reading *People*. Invariably, as we all do, she'd make comments about this or that celebrity. During the whole process, I couldn't help but notice that Anne kept giving Laura dirty looks.

After I finished with Anne, Laura hopped up on the bed for her turn. At some point during the waxing, Laura—who has a very low pain threshold—asked Anne, "Aren't you going to hold my hand, honey?'

Anne readily replied, "Nope. When I was going through the same pain, you were reading about Britney Spears. Now, suffer!" She grabbed the same magazine and started to flip through its pages. A little later, though, she was comforting Laura and we all laughed a little at the cute couple dynamics between them.

❦

I also see plenty of gay men come through my studio. It's a totally different experience. At the risk of sounding stereotypical, it is amazing how much I learn about cooking, gardening, and interior decoration whenever these guys get talking!

One gay client in particular, James, is a travel agent who throws great parties at his home in the Oakland Hills. He comes to me to get rid of the hair on his back and buttocks, and he always teaches me something new.

James sees me regularly, not only for waxing, but also for facials. I joke that the facials are a good thing, because I see way too much of his backside and not enough of his handsome face. We've developed a comfortable friendship, and I love being on his party guest list.

James' home décor would easily make the cover of any decorating magazine. I always love to browse through his house when I'm there so I can take notes of his latest innovative ideas. Once, at a New Year's party, he had a beautiful arrangement in the downstairs bathroom. It was a vase containing three Bird of Paradise stalks held up with beach sand. He'd placed the vase in the middle of a glass plate and surrounded it with little lavender candles. It looked magical! The dim candlelight and the lavender smell with those vibrant flowers were a great combination. I never could've come up with that on my own. But you can bet I copied it at my next dinner party!

At one point, I was thinking about redoing the chairs in my dining room and couldn't for the life of me settle on a specific color scheme or fabric choice. I mentioned this to James, and he suggested that I browse through some fabric stores. But that didn't help since I couldn't make up my mind. I was so frustrated with myself.

A few days later, James showed up with a few fabric samples and a window treatment that he himself had designed. I chose a beautiful sage–colored fabric for the chairs, and I liked it so much I decided to use it for the windows, too. After that, James suggested I paint the walls a light avocado color, which, of course, I did. I never question James! Needless to say, all my friends love my new dining room. I just smile when they tell me what great decorating sense I have and how fabulous it all looks. Which proves my point: my clients enrich my life as much as I do theirs.

❧

Every year around Christmas I try to find a little token to thank each of my clients for all the trust they instill in me. I want to let them know I appreciate them and that I recognize that it takes a lot of confidence to let me powder, rip, and inflict temporary pain on one of the most sensitive parts of their bodies. I find it easier to give the same present to everyone, and I usually hand it out when I am done with their December appointment.

One memorable gift I came up with was a tiny red bow and a Santa's hat. The idea was for them to place the bow in their pubic area, just above the landing strip, and wear Santa's hat—and *only* the Santa's hat, welcoming their partners home with a Ho! Ho! Ho! The response was a roaring success.

Jennie's husband, after learning that it was my idea, started to shout, "Reny for President! Reny for President!" while still in bed.

❧

Marcy's husband left a message on my machine saying that was the cleverest gift his wife had ever received and that he wished it had been his idea. He said she looked so beautiful naked with just the bow and the hat on, and added how happy he was about the role I play in his wife's life.

❧

Lisa K. called from a hotel in Palm Springs just to tell me that she and her boyfriend were having a great time and that he took pictures of her in the "outfit" I'd given her so I could see. She sounded a little drunk, and I'm sure they were really having fun.

❧

Patricia sent me a Christmas card, and in it she said her husband brought the red bow to work so he could glue it to the picture of her on his desk. He was calling her at home more often now that the small item was there to remind him of the "hot" Christmas night they'd had.

Carla blames me for causing her husband to chase her around the house. She says that he can't stop talking about Reny's gift, Reny's gift....

During Deana's next visit she mentioned that now, whenever she wants something done around the house, all she has to do is to be wearing Santa's hat when her husband arrives home from work.

Happy Holidays!

"Oh Reny I am so happy, so happy to be here. I almost had a seizure every time I looked at my hairy poosie."
Sarah W. as she was getting undressed for the waxing.

The Senior Crowd

If you think bikini waxing is just for the young, hot, skinny ones, let me remind you that sex gets better as we age. And nobody knows more about that subject than my "mature" clientele.

Take Jean as an example: she's been my client for over four years. She has four grandchildren and works at Macy's in the lingerie department. She usually comes in to wax her brows, legs, and just the regular bikini line. One fall, before going to the Caribbean to celebrate her thirtieth wedding anniversary, she came as usual, and we did the usual bikini wax. After I was done, she jumped off the bed and looked at herself in the big mirror. I was puzzled by her gesture and asked if there was anything wrong.

She said, "No," and in a low tone of voice added, "I was just wondering how the BBW would look on me. I think that after thirty years with the same man, he wouldn't mind me doing something wild; what do you think?"

As usual, I said it was her decision and she replied, "Let's go to Brazil, girl!" Then, she jumped back on the bed. As I had her spread and lift her legs, I kept waiting for some sign of embarrassment but that didn't happen. When I was all finished, she looked at herself again in the mirror. This time she said, "I can't wait to see my husband's face when he sees my BBW."

Needless to say I, too, was dying to know how he would react. A week later, I received a postcard from her Caribbean resort saying, *Total success! Sex is better after the Brazilian—*

schedule me at the regular time in three weeks!

I couldn't help but think that despite how busy life is with work and family, and with all the challenges we face as we age, there are always ways to spice up our relationships with our men. It can be a night at the movies, dinner out, or a getaway where you can really put that BBW to good use.

Another sassy senior, Jullienne is sixty-two years young and full of life. She's been happily married for over thirty years, and has four sons and three grandsons. She works as a special education teacher, takes salsa-dancing lessons, and is learning Italian. I've known Julienne now for almost four years and still to this day I am always in awe of how beautiful she looks at her age. She has dark skin, huge green eyes, and beautiful black hair.

Looking at her figure and features now I can only wonder how vibrant she must have been in her younger years. She is pleasant with always a nice word to say and a ready smile. And she's proud to say that she is still "one hundred percent intact" as far as plastic surgery goes. Lately, though, she's been saying that she's considering some "improvements" in her near future and has been starting to talk about things like the best time of the year to get under the knife and how to go about saving money for surgery.

Last month she called me asking to change her appointment time. Luckily I had just what she wanted available. She exclaimed, "Oh, Reny, you are so good to me, thank you so much!"

My only response was, "What are you talking about? You drive twenty-five miles to come to see me, I apply hot wax on your poosie and rip it off, inflicting pain on your most private parts, and on top of all that, I still charge you. And then you tell me I am soooo good to you? I cannot imagine what those people who are not so good to you do!"

"I can't wait to tell my husband that one," she said, laughing.

At the rescheduled appointment time, Julienne showed up with this devilish smile on her pretty face. When I asked her what was going on, she said that for many years her husband had been begging her to go on a nude resort in Mexico. Since she'd always been very hairy down there she always felt too self-conscious. But now, after having "gone Brazilian" and learning how to feel more comfortable in showing herself off, she finally told him yes. While in Mexico she proud about the fact that she finally overcame her inner fears of exposing herself on a nude beach. Once again, she proved my point: it's never too late to be adventurous, especially after a good waxing job!

Speaking of adventurous, can you imagine being single in your fifties?

My client Tricia is, and I get to hear all about it. Despite sensitive skin that shows some lines, it's her energy that fools you into thinking she's much younger. Tricia is a petite blond with huge blue eyes. She's been divorced now for three years and, thanks to a fat alimony agreement, has no need to join the workforce.

During her appointments I get to hear all about her self-indulgent lifestyle and dating adventures. One was her affair with a gorgeous, married man she met while flying first class. (It ended in classic fashion, with her fleeing a hotel room, leaving clothing behind when his wife showed up unexpectedly). Another time she bought a pair of $700 pumps, which made me gasp! But, as all good shopaholics would say, she "had to have them." After she told me that, I stopped in my tracks for a minute, and she asked me "What are you thinking?"

I told her that I was trying to figure out how many poosies I'd have to wax in order to buy such expensive shoes. On the other hand, I confess that sometimes I envy some aspects of her life as a single woman. Not having to report to anybody, being able to make her own decisions without the approval of anyone else, to own her time, to travel extensively anywhere...that can be an interesting way to lead your life.

Many times she has asked me, "C'mon, Reny, come with me and the girls, let's go to Italy. It's just for three weeks."

I always answer with another question. "How can I go somewhere for so long, knowing that I'll be leaving so many hairy poosies behind?" Undoubtedly, it would be great, but unlike Tricia, I do have to work for a living.

Well, last weekend I gave in a little and went out to dinner with Tricia and two other girlfriends. Afterwards, they all start to talk about going dancing somewhere. I was tired and said I'd rather go home. Tricia quickly said, "Oh, no. You drove with me and you are coming with us. I'll drive you home later."

Ack! She had driven me there, hadn't she? And she wasn't going to go out of her way to please me; I was stuck. So we all went to this "hot spot" where you'll find lots of 50-something people dressed like they are in denial over their lost youth but still looking for love.

As we were looking for a place to sit, this tall blond man grabbed my arm and led me to the dance floor. He started to talk and I almost got sick from his fetid breath. Before the music was over I excused myself and was making my way towards the girls when another short guy took my hand. Once again, I found myself on the dance floor. He started to talk, saying (probably to impress me) that he was a very successful plastic surgeon and that my nose was perfect. As a matter of fact, he went on to say, "That's what we as doctors try to achieve when performing a nose job. You have the perfect nose!"

Jokingly, I asked him if he would like me being a "nose model" for his brochures, and he said he would. Then he offered to buy me a drink, saying the bar owner was a friend and client of his. I thanked him but refused, saying that I didn't want anything. He was surprised by my answer and insisted that he at least get me a glass of wine. While he walked to the bar, I tried to escape to where the girls were. I was almost there when a tall, almost-good-looking guy asked me to dance. The girls were laughing at me at this point, and off to dance I went. It wasn't a slow song, but he grabbed me anyway and, within a few seconds, I started to feel his hard, um, instrument rubbing against my thigh. Offended, I pushed him away and, surprising myself, said in a very loud and firm voice, "Do you want to dance or do you want to fuck? I am here to dance."

Well, he surely wasn't expecting *that* reaction. To his credit, he apologized profusely and by the time he was done, so was the song. After that incident I asked Tricia to drive me home. I was definitely tired now.

While getting ready for bed (yes, I do wash my face and apply moisturizer religiously), I was thinking about Tricia and her friends. It seemed that what they were looking for was someone to replace that empty hole that was once filled with love, romance, and the fulfillment of desires. Despite all the freedom they say they are happy to have, the need for companionship and the fear of aging alone is real. We all crave having someone special in our lives one way or another, at some point or another.

The reality is that it may take a long time until Tricia and her friends find someone with the qualities they are looking for. Unfortunately for some people—the ones who are especially eager to have someone in their lives—the rush can cloud their judgment. This is a recipe for disaster and can continue and in endless negative cycle. I just hope they do find their Mr. Rights and live happily ever after.

Getting into bed with my sound-asleep husband, I felt so fortunate to have my man of twenty years next to me. So what if my time is not my own? So what if I can't go on exotic vacations with my girlfriends? Even though I have to answer to him sometimes, even with all the ups and downs of marriage and the constant worry about my children's whereabouts, after that night I could honestly say: I love my life!

BBW Quickies

Anne gets her BBW every three weeks, at her husband Harold's request. During one appointment, I decided to go the extra mile for good old Harry, waxing beyond the usual amount.

Later Anne told me about his reaction:

"I think I met Reny in a previous life. How else would you explain the fact that she knows exactly what I like?"

Ladies with an attitude,
fellows that are in the mood...
Madonna

Unique Ladies

Charlie is a crossdresser. He's sixty-four years old and the skin under his eyes is so baggy, it reminds me of a pair of soggy, wet Band-Aids. His blue eyes contrast very well with his dark skin, though, and I can see how handsome— or pretty?—he once was. He has a gentle spirit and I can hardly imagine him being angry, raising his voice, or having his feathers ruffled by anyone. And I do know he wears feathers! He speaks with a soft voice that underscores his unusual sweetness.

He often tells me how much he loves to come to get waxed, not only because of the smoothness of his body afterwards, but also because the two of us have fun together. Throughout the years we have developed a lovely friendship that goes beyond the waxing room. We meet at the gym a few times a week and often grab a bite to eat together afterwards. A widower, Charlie feels lonely sometimes, and I know he looks forward to his appointments. Knowing that he's always in the mood to vent, I've learned to reserve more time than normal for his appointments.

Charlie is very well read, and he delights me with the fact that I can ask him about anything. He always has the right answer as well as something interesting to add to any subject. Besides being a wonderful listener, he enchants me with his stories, which can range from the subject in the book he read last to the transvestite bar he visited over the weekend.

One of tenets of the waxer/waxee relationship is

knowing how to open enough space for people to share their lives, without appearing nosy or intrusive. So, since it's none of my business, I never asked him why or how he became a crossdresser. I figured he'd let me know if and when he decided to. Finally, one day when we were talking about life as a rollercoaster ride, he willingly launched into the subject. He told me that he'd been drafted into the Army during World War II at the age of sixteen, a time when many boys start to explore their sexuality. But the Army has a way of repressing people. When Charlie came back five years later, he met a woman at a friend's house and within a year, Charlie and Anita got married and began to raise a family. A few years later, he found himself alone in the house folding the laundry. When he came across some of his wife's stockings, he felt a curiosity so strong that he put them on. He found he liked the feeling of it. He then went to his wife's closet and tried one of her dresses. He said he was amazed with the great feeling of wearing women's clothes: he felt complete.

As time went on, Charlie secretly started to check out crossdressers' clubs and other events announced by his genre's magazine, *LadyLike*. He felt at home from the first time he went, and he made a few friends that led to a life full of new discoveries.

All sorts of hidden feelings from his teen years started to come out in a big way. He went on to tell me that, for years, he would leave his wigs, dresses, shoes, and makeup at a friend's house and often found excuses to go out at night to the clubs.

This was all hidden from his wife. The friend—we'll call him Alex—is a very well known OB-GYN in our community. He has the perfect excuse for getting away to his crossdresser's parties. He claims that he's on call and his wife Kendra has no choice but to stay home with their two girls, patiently waiting for him to come home exhausted from "another long night at the hospital."

Another of Charlie's friends is Paul, who has since become a client, along with his wife Nay. This Silicon Valley executive is one of the lucky ones; Nay approves of his "hobby." She talks naturally about Paul's desire to dress as a woman and even encourages him to go out, helping him choose the best wig or the right makeup. She tells me that they wait anxiously for Halloween so that Paul can be in the spotlight, enjoying the attention he craves all year long. "Some men play golf, others spend time in bars, many like to watch sports. Paul loves to dress as a woman, so what?" Nay told me once. One can only imagine what their sex life is like, or what sorts of things go on in the privacy of their own home. But there's something to be said about a relationship that secure. Their marriage vows should have said, "...in sickness and health, in men's or women's clothes, till death do us part." However it works, it works for them. It's a really unique way of life and I give Nay tons of credit for being a strong enough woman to support her husband's choice of leisure activities.

Finally, one weekend Charlie's wife had asked him to accompany her to Macy's. Surprised, he asked her why she wanted him to go with her since she always shopped by herself. She turned to him and said, "I want to buy you some stockings so you'll stop putting holes in mine!" His jaw dropped, and she hugged him saying that she knew about his outings and about his love for dressing like a woman, and that it was okay with her. As he told me this, he started to cry, saying how much he loved her and how much he missed her. I hugged him then, and he thanked me for listening.

More often than not, Charlie comes to his waxing appointment in men's attire, but whenever he's meeting any crossdresser friends for lunch, he shows up dressed as Charlene (his female counterpart). Needless to say, I couldn't contain myself the first time he came in drag. I remember the Marilyn Monroe wig, the tacky makeup, the cheap jewelry, the white stockings, the tight black skirt, and the high heels. The heels caught my attention first, not because they were different or anything, but because of how Charlie was trying to balance and teeter on them. Since this was so new to me, it took me a second to get over the initial shock. But I had every intention of letting Charlie—or, Charlene—know I accepted hi—I mean, her, so I managed to tell him/her how lovely she/he looked. Oh, forget it. He was so proud of his makeup and his new purse (which he'd bought at Nordstrom on sale—go, girl!). His happiness was infectious.

After the waxing he got dressed again, and I tactfully showed him how to walk in heels. "Keep your legs straight; don't move them or you may fall. Walk firmly, confidently, and don't forget to move your hips to look sexier." He demonstrated for me, loving the idea of moving his hips.

A few weeks later, I started getting calls from the crossdressers' club where Charlie is a member. They all needed waxing done. Currently, I have over fifteen crossdresser clients. And they all insist on being called not Paul, but Paulette; not John, but Joanna; not Rick, but Suzette. It took me a while to get used to the names, but they are all very unique ladies and I always look forward to their appointments.

One Man, Two Men, Three Men...Gee

"All five of my boyfriends love my BBW," my client Nadia told me one day. I did a double take, not sure I had heard the number correctly. Let's face it, most of us can barely handle one man. I can't imagine five! I guess I could see the benefit of having two boyfriends simultaneously; in case one dumps you, it'd be good to have another on reserve. But five? I mean, really, that's just too many penises to keep track of.

Nadia is thirty-one years old with long black hair, dark eyes, and a beautiful smile. She's no Jennifer Lopez, but she is one of those people who gets noticed as soon as they enter a room. Nadia is in sales and travels often for business—which, ultimately, is her secret for collecting all those boyfriends. She is the modern day sailor-woman, except instead of a woman in every port she has a boyfriend in each town.

During one appointment, Nadia asked about what sorts of waxing specialties I offered. Some women like to "shape" their hairline into, say, a heart or an animal. Think of it as sculpting or decorative hedge work. I was inspired to start offering this service to my clients after I saw a woman in Brazil that had designed a Christmas tree in her sister's poosie. It was amazing, worth showing anybody, really. I told Nadia I could design anything as long as she had enough hair for the shape of the figure.

The most requested shape is the heart on Valentine's Day. The Playboy Strip that is just a fine line of hair in the center of the pubic area is also popular. The Beyond Brazilian, where all the hair is removed leaving nothing but smooth skin, is often—believe it or not—requested by middle-aged women. Initials of boyfriend's names are also requested. In Nadia's case, the initials were about the only thing she could not do due to the multitude of names. If you think about it, that could have generated some serious problems. She agreed with me about the lettering, and that was that.

To my surprise, though, she came soon after and requested the letter G. Puzzled, I asked, "What would her U.S. based boyfriends Bob, Marcus, Juan, and Bryan say?"

With a half-coy smile on her face she told me about her upcoming two-month business/vacation trip to Italy, where she was to spend a month in the south with a "Giacomo" and a month in the north with a "Gino." Since the hair grows back in four to five weeks, she had calculated that by the time she returned to the U.S., the hair would have grown in again, hiding the letter completely; the other men would be clueless.

Now, that's what I call strategic planning—she took into account growth management and calculated her time and resources perfectly.

T is for TONY

Natalie is one of my favorite people in the whole world. She's a tall, robust—dare I say big-boned?—girl with what some people call "childbearing hips." She's solid as a rock. And she always has this fresh look, as if she just got out of the shower.

Our personalities just mesh. We agree about practically everything from politics to nutrition. We love eating well, so we share recipes. Gardening is a hobby for both of us, so we share planting tips with each other. Occasionally, when I have time, we schedule her appointment for just before lunch so we can go out together afterwards.

Last year for her boyfriend Tony's birthday, she decided to go the extra mile for him. They were taking a trip to Vegas for the weekend, and she requested that I wax her poosie hair into the shape of the letter T.

To do this right and make it look really great, I have to remove all the hair on the butt cheeks and labia in addition to the parts of the pubic area, which need to be removed to make the desired shape. After that's done, I tweeze the extra hair above the poosie in order to really make the letter sharp. Letters are time consuming due to all the tweezing, and since I am a perfectionist, I take the necessary time. I use a magnifying lamp to remove even the hairs not visible to the naked eye. We all agree that tweezing sucks, but it allows my clients to have a hair-free poosie for a longer period of time.

After I was all done with Natalie's T it looked fabulous! She couldn't get over it and gave me a hug, saying, "Thank you for the work of art."

I can't take all the credit for how great she looked. Not all of us (or our poosies) were created equal and, as far letters and shapes go, they usually look better on a wider-hipped woman like Natalie.

A week later I received a thank you card from Nat telling me that Tony was beside himself with what she had done for him. He even proposed to her during their Las Vegas weekend! She said that it was all because of the letter T.

Well, I am modest and would like to hope that he proposed to her because he loved her and because it was time. They'd been together for three years already. Maybe the letter T just gave him that extra dose of courage he needed in order to take the big step toward marriage.

Last June, Nat and Tony were married in Lake Tahoe. It was a beautiful outdoor ceremony. I was honored to be there with my husband, so happy for the two of them.

During dinner we were seated with several other couples at a big round table. As we were introducing ourselves, I felt like a celebrity. When I said my name they all became so friendly and awestruck. As I suspected, very soon the conversation turned to my career.

Turns out Tony had mentioned the letter T to some of his buddies (what guy wouldn't?), and they were all wondering if their wives would go for it. After a few bottles of wine they became even more straightforward in their questions. Even the wives loosened up and got interested in the subject. They all wanted my business card and were asking about the different shapes I could design. Two of the couples were none too happy about my answer when I told them the only letters I wouldn't do were M and W. (They're just too difficult, with all those points.) Their husbands' names? Mike and Walter.

Clients with Benefits

Okay, I confess: I speed. Not too much, mind you—perhaps just a wee five mph above the speed limit. Well, maybe seven. I am one of those drivers with one eye on the road and the other on the speedometer. So I wasn't surprised last year when I was pulled over by a policeman on a nearby side street after dropping my son Mitchell at school. I was en route to work when I saw the lights flashing in my rearview mirror and got that feeling in the pit of my stomach. You know the one. The officer sidled up to my car and said those three little words: "License and registration." After he checked my documents, he asked me if I knew how fast I was going—as if I wanted to know. I mean, I assumed that if he stopped me it was because I was speeding, so I wished he'd just give me the ticket and let me go.

I said I had no idea but that I was late for work. He then walked towards the back of the car and came back asking, "What kind of license plate is this?—(heart)WAXING."

I told him that I wax people for a living and that he was actually making me late for a client who was probably sitting there waiting for me at the shop. Ignoring my comment, he asked, "What kind of waxing?"

Why is it that every time a guy sees the word waxing, they immediately think about a shiny sports car instead of a human body? "Body. Body wax, body parts," I told him.

To my astonishment, he asked for my business card. Immediately I said, "I'll trade my business card for my driver's license." He handed my license back, saying, "Please don't ever tell anyone that I did this, but you can go. I'll call you for an appointment. You have a nice day."

I could not believe my good fortune! I was so happy that I couldn't contain myself. No traffic school, no fees, no grief from my husband? What a difference a license plate makes!

Needless to say, I was delighted when Officer Louis showed up for his appointment. He'd been a Good Samaritan and it was my turn to reciprocate. When I opened the door and saw him in his "off-duty" clothes I remember thinking he looked much cuter in his uniform. On the other hand, along with his uniform went his cop attitude.

Citizen Louis was very pleasant and I was captivated by his glowing smile. After all, smiling is something cops don't seem to do at all while at work. Louis requested I wax his back and chest, and I couldn't help noticing his perfect physique: six-pack abs, a trim waist, and those "handles" on his hips like the statue of David. Oh, sometimes my job is so rough. Just in the middle of my dreamy observations, he snapped me back to reality by telling me that his girlfriend was coming to visit from Toronto and that he wanted to surprise her with a sheen torso.

During a series of appointments I learned a lot about

Louis's chosen career. For starters, being a police officer is a thankless job. No thank-you cards, pats on the back, or even kind words. Cops basically do what they are supposed to do, and that's it; they are somewhat anonymous.

What's more, Louis often has to work the graveyard shift, which is extremely high risk. A long night in the patrol car during "the witching hours," combined with the lack of sleep, which can cloud judgment, makes the potential for danger much greater than during the daytime. The sleep deprivation, along with on-the-job stress, is responsible for a multitude of health problems and can cause strain on interpersonal relationships.

Louis gave me some insight into the quotas he must meet monthly for traffic tickets. It's not as simple as it seems. Just writing the ticket is not the end of the process. If the driver decides to dispute the violation, the officer needs to show up in court and face that driver. This often ends up being a laborious occupation.

Out of all the line-of-duty hardships, he told me that handcuffing a mother or father and taking them away in front of their children is the most difficult part of his job. My heart melted when he said that, and I could see beyond the tough guy exterior into the human, sweet side of him.

More than once, Louis has invited me to ride along and watch what goes on at night, but I've repeatedly declined. Knowing myself, I just can't imagine sleeping soundly ever again if I were to see a dead person or someone getting shot.

By Louis giving me just a glimpse into his world every month, though, I've learned to admire the officer and the citizen Louis. Very often, people tell me they find my line of work a "difficult" job. But I disagree, since I love doing it.

And it's all relative. There are so many dangerous jobs out there. Perhaps because of what I know now, I think being a cop has to be one of the hardest. And for that, Louis will always get my infinite respect.

Bragging in Style

stress [stres] n. —physical, mental, or emotional strain
or tension; worry

Doctors tend to explain away any ailment they cannot diagnose by calling it stress. Some people use stress as an excuse for anything they can't or don't want to do. There is no doubt that people today are stressed. I just don't enjoy the misuse of the word.

As someone who grew up poor, I dealt with plenty of adversity. I learned how to be practical, how to deal with everyday "stress" as a fact of life. But stress, in my dictionary, has a deeper meaning. It's when you feel helpless watching someone you love dealing with a terminal illness or being unable to feed your own children.

Shuttling kids around in a Suburban with AC, pop-down DVD players, and seat-warmers is not stress in my book. I've heard people say "It's all relative," but I would love for those people to walk a mile in someone else's shoes.

As a professional who has gained the trust of many, I often listen to my clients' complaints. Sometimes I stand there in utter disbelief. I can't help thinking they have no idea how good they have it.

Kelly is a fifty-nine-year-old brunette who spends her days either shopping or lunching with friends. She is slender with short, spiky hair. Despite the fact that she has three grown boys, she wears her pants with a very low rise, showing her pierced belly button. These are the pants teenagers wear nowadays. To me, they just don't look right on a woman pushing sixty.

Kelly is also very rich, and visits her plastic surgeon at least once a year. A Botox application here, a nip and a tuck there... She jokes about it by saying, "I've had so many Botox applications, even my clothes are wrinkle free!"

Each time Kelly shows up for an appointment, no matter what she does or how well everything is going in her life, she always reports that she is "extremely stressed." This stress of hers comes from various sources. One day she arrived looking truly exhausted. When I asked her what happened she replied, "Oh, I just had to sign this huge stack of papers for the sale of my house."

Later on in the visit she mentioned the price: a cool 2.3 million. Oh, what some folks would give for that kind of stress! On another occasion Kelly complained that she was going through a hard time. You see, she couldn't decide what to bring with her on her upcoming trip to the Caribbean. *If you only knew,* I thought.

People like Kelly aren't really complaining, they're bragging in style. I listen to all of them—I know that it's a part of my job—but I can't help thinking how much I'd love to take Kelly to Brazil or to any Third World country.

I would have her spend a few weeks traveling around, just watching the way people live in those places. I'd show her how hard it is to wash clothes by hand, piece by piece; how tiring it is to walk eight blocks to the supermarket and walk back carrying the grocery bags—how when you arrive home you have deep marks in your hands from the bags. She'd learn what it's like to use herbs to cure your child from an ailment because you can't afford the doctor's appointment, or how creative you have to be to transform and preserve today's leftovers because you don't know if tomorrow there will be anything else to feed your kids. I wonder if that would teach her the real meaning of stress.

During one appointment, after I'd finished her BBW, Kelly asked me if I wouldn't mind tweezing the gray hairs from her poosie. This is a laborious process, as the hairs have to be isolated and tweezed one by one. I suddenly had a flashback to those days of washing clothes piece by piece and, before I knew it, I heard myself saying, "I don't have the two hours it would take to do that. And besides, I'm not sure if you really want a bald poosie!"

She looked at me, shocked by my answer. Remembering the way another client had once described her 'more salt than pepper' pubic hairs, I added, "Welcome to the Richard Gere Club, honey," transforming her scowl into a smile.

After she left I wondered what she would do next. Maybe at home she told her husband how stressed she was over her poosie turning gray. If she asks me again, maybe I'll tweeze it—but for now, let her stress over it.

BBW Quickies

Just recently I attended a fundraiser dinner for which I donated a BBW gift certificate. The certificate was a great addition to an enormous spa basket and part of the evening auction.

As the auction started, the bids slowly went up until a friend asked me to mention the BBW gift certificate inside of it. For a while I refused his request, but finally, just for the fun of it I got up and in a loud voice announced,

"Hey guys, there's a BBW gift certificate in the basket."

The response was immediate; the husbands' bids hit five hundred dollars to everyone's surprise (including mine) and for the fundraiser's delight.

Aging Gracefully? No Way!

Ana Cristina has been a client since I started this business almost a decade ago. I vividly remember her first BBW (and I'm sure she does, too!). Her poosie was so hairy it looked more like a shag carpet than a Persian rug. The appointment was long, but at the end the transformation was so dramatic, I started thinking about getting a Polaroid camera so I could take before and after pictures. I could just see the brochure: a "tarantula" on the left and the clean poosie on the right, just like in a plastic surgeon's office. But I never got around to it. Who knows how many willing models I would have had.

Ana Cristina is a pretty, forty-five-year old woman, and despite four pregnancies, her body is still nice-looking. She told me she goes to the gym whenever she can—"So I can get some energy to face the day with the rug rats," she'd say.

Our conversations always center on family matters, mostly kids, and girls' nights out. These ladies-only events are something she takes pleasure from and, to be honest, I think she deserves it after minding the kids every day, all week.

It surprised me one day when our conversation turned to plastic surgery and I found out how opposed to it Ana Cristina was. After all our time together, it had never come up. Around that time, her good friend Anita was planning to go for a tummy tuck and breast reduction, which Ana Cristina thought was "shallow." We started discussing the choices people make in the name of vanity.

"I can't believe that she'll be spending all this money on herself when she has three little kids and could save all this money for their college years," Ana Cristina remarked.

My response was, "Honey, one thing has nothing to do with the other. Since her kids are still little she'll have time to save money after paying for her surgery. After all, money is just money. You work, you earn it, you spend it, you work more, and you get more. Besides, who can predict the future?"

It's funny how, even though I didn't know Anita, I jumped to her defense. But let's face it, who knows what Anita's kids will end up doing when they reach college age? Their mom is focusing on the present, and right now all she wants is to feel good about herself. I went on to tell Ana Cristina that I thought it was a very personal and difficult decision to make, and that many times friends need their friends' support when they're about to "go under the knife," as they say.

That only vain or shallow people get plastic surgery is a stigma that sounds absurd to me. If Anita had the choice to improve her self-esteem, if she could afford it, and if she was brave enough to do it, I say, "You go, girl, and enjoy the results."

"We all have our priorities in life,' I added to Ana Cristina. "Yours may not be a tummy tuck because your body shape is different than Anita's, but who knows? A few years from now, those wrinkles around your eyes may start to bother you and you might change your opinion."

Well, now I was really getting carried away. To her credit,

Ana Cristina listened intently for a while and, although the conversation got a little intense at points, she didn't leave fuming like she was when we started. And we are still friends.

While to some age isn't a major concern, to others being asked about their age is as insulting as if they were being asked how often they have sex or how much money they make. When you are in your twenties you consider forty old, but as you approach that age your opinion starts to change and you look for ways to appear younger, reverse the clock. It's only natural.

I remember that, just before I turned forty, I started thinking about going gray, letting my wrinkles show how much laughter I had had in life, and being happy to disclose my age as if it was public record. But, just before that fateful date, I realized that I really didn't feel my age. I felt happy and young on the inside, but the exterior layer was a different story and I decided it needed some work.

Many years ago when I was contemplating going for my tummy tuck. I talked to my personal trainer about my abs. Despite the hundreds of crunches I was doing each time, I still couldn't see any improvement in my stomach area. He gently grabbed the loose skin around my belly and said, kindly, "You have a six pack underneath all this; not much more we can do here at the gym." Ack!

The next day I looked at myself in the mirror. Having been thin all my life, I still had skinny arms and skinny legs, but now there was this belly sticking out. I looked like a worm that had swallowed an olive pit, or a mother kangaroo with a hanging pouch. Any top I wore had to be long and wide in order to cover my flabby belly. A big tummy can really destroy a silhouette, and I was getting tired of working so hard to cover it up.

Still, I had some reservations about my decision. I felt I needed some assurance, a positive comment about the procedure, a happy-ending story that would make me grab the phone and go for it. That same week I got my answer. When my client Caroline came for her appointment I noticed a certain glow on her face. She was wearing a body-conscious dress and high heels, and I noticed that her waist was much smaller. I couldn't help myself; I had to stare. When I remarked on how she got herself looking so great, she said, "Oh, I was just tired of carrying the extra pounds, and two months ago I had a tummy tuck." She looked terrific!

Needless to say, that following week I met with her plastic surgeon. He agreed with my personal trainer that there was nothing more I could do to get rid of the six pounds—yes, six pounds—of extra skin in my abdominal area. Still, after my first consultation I deliberated for a few weeks. Finally, after talking to more women who had done it successfully and without regret, I handed my plastic card to my plastic surgeon and told him, "Let's do it!"

I'm happy to report that the results are incredible. I no longer have those rolls of fat spilling out of my jeans—the muffin top—and I dropped from a size 12 to a size 6. I feel more confident about myself; I no longer dread clothes shopping, and some days I even feel I could win a Miss Universe contest!

It's amazing after you've had a tummy tuck, how many women you find that come out of the woodwork, wanting to talk openly about it. So far I have not met a single woman who regrets having one done, pain and expense aside. What

I do get, though, are people asking me, "Was it painful?" My response is always, "Yes, but so were my three labors, so is a migraine. So is any other pain you feel in life. But women are tough and resilient and we have energy reserves for situations like these."

But every once in a while I do come across other women just like Ana Cristina, vehemently opposed to plastic surgery. Doris is one of these clients. She is in her forties with a good figure and beautiful skin. She has a beautiful smile, but I have to say her laughter is a little annoying to me. It is loud and strident, like a pile of porcelain dishes breaking. She had heard about my surgery and asked me how I was feeling, was I happy with the recovery, etc.

"It wasn't too bad, and I am in love with my new body!" I said with enthusiasm.

Doris just looked at me. "You looked good to me before and I really can't understand why you had to put your body through all that ordeal. We should be kind to ourselves. We should age naturally, not push it."

I couldn't believe my ears! After the few seconds it took to compose myself, I replied, "You may be right about that, but don't forget that we're all entitled to our own choices. I did what I thought was right for me, and I am very pleased about it." My chest was so tight I could barely breathe.

I went on by saying, "Here's a question for you. If you think women should age naturally, why are you here getting waxed? Why do you wax your legs, eyebrows, lip, and armpits? Why do you color your hair? Should you not just keep your natural gray? Also, why do you do a manicure and pedicure?" I'm said this very sweetly all the while, mind you.

My accent helps me be a little feistier when I want to be. "But, really, Doris, if you went 'all natural,' you'd look like a cave woman!"

Poor Doris tried to mumble something, but I cut her off. I was on a roll. "And one more thing. In order for somebody to have plastic surgery there are two important things you need to have: guts and money. Now, roll over so I can wax the back of your legs. We want you to look pretty, don't we?"

The Prozac Puppy

Françoise is a tall and sophisticated woman. The daughter of a wealthy family, she has kept herself well maintained through the years—her hair, dress, and shoes are always in perfect unison. To this day, after two years of waxing her, I still smile watching her walk toward my front door. Françoise screams fashion from head to toe; complete with French poodle in hand.

Françoise' first visit was a memorable one for me. I get used to clients being shy, sometimes even refusing to open their legs. And I had pegged Françoise for that modest type. Therefore, I was stunned to see how fast she undressed and jumped onto the bed, spreading her legs open with her feet high in the air. Modesty? What modesty? She was ready to roll and it showed. But all that time saved was eaten up because Françoise had been shaving, and her hair wasn't quite long enough to be waxed.

In this situation, I remove what can be removed with wax, and then I tweeze the remaining hair. This always turns a quick visit into a lengthy one. But Françoise was patient, and pleased with the results. At the end of the session she said, '*Cherie*, my husband will have sushi for dinner tonight!'

"Do you really know how to make sushi from scratch?" I asked.

She just smiled and pointed down to her sheen poosie. We both laughed.

The rich, like any community, come in many colors as far as personality is concerned. In Françoise' case, she is wealthy but bored. She's always complaining that there is nothing to do. Perhaps it's her French existentialism. One visit, after I sat there hearing once again about how little she had going on, I suggested that she look into doing something useful such as volunteering for a cause or working part-time. My thought was to put her endless years of education, good personality, and resources to use while at the same time preventing her from, as she said, "being alone at her McMansion feeling blue."

We even talked about how having children would make her happy and really change her life. Unfortunately she and her husband had been trying unsuccessfully for a few years. Well, after our little chat, I guess she settled for the canine breed because the next time I saw her she had acquired her now ever-present French poodle.

One day Françoise showed up with her poodle, "Petite Princesse," in a well-decorated basket. She told me she had thought a lot about our previous conversation and felt she really needed something to care for. This was far from what I'd meant when I suggested she get busy, but alas, self-care means different things to different people, and I am glad acquiring Princesse made Françoise feel better.

Undoubtedly French, this diva dog was maybe eight or nine inches long and weighed a mere three to four pounds. Françoise seemed so happy and couldn't stop talking about her new "baby." Princesse was definitely pampered; she arrived at my office once wearing a Gucci sweater and smelling like she had just come out of a spa. Françoise told me that Petite Princesse was very intelligent and they had bonded intensely since she'd gotten her. Toy dogs are well known for bonding generally with one person, the one that pampers and pleases them the most, and Petite Princesse was no exception.

Over the next few visits I learned more about Françoise' dog and the way she was cared for. Françoise told me her *chou chou* (a French term of affection) had decided to sleep between her and her husband and that the dog refused to eat from a bowl, waiting instead for Françoise to feed her by hand!

Once Françoise went to a pet store for snacks for the princess. As the clerk walked her to the aisle carrying dog treats, he showed her some peanut butter nibbles. Upon seeing this, Françoise replied, "Oh, no, no, *cherie*, I am raising her as a French puppy and I need some pate snacks for her." Well, she was none too happy when the man said they didn't carry pate snacks. Very much against her will, Françoise bought the peanut butter (at least they were *organique*!) and decided that on her next trip to Paris she would buy true French snacks for her deserving Petit Princesse.

But life is always full of surprises. One day, Françoise called me to announce that she had finally gotten pregnant. We talked about the fact that having the puppy must have distracted her from all the pressure of wanting a baby. Nature, with all its wonders, had worked its magic.

For the next nine months I saw Petite Princesse grow right along with Françoise' belly, and the following spring Evelyne was born. I am now able to see another side to Françoise. With no more time to complain about boredom, she is alert, happy, and always on the go. And, not surprisingly, she looks prettier than ever, with a smile on her face all the time. But Françoise' life was not the only one to change with baby's arrival. Mine did, too.

These days, Françoise' visits are hectic, and I try to work as fast as I can. Very often, baby Evelyne wakes up in the middle of a waxing session and we place her on Mom's chest while I finish the job. During one visit, she had the baby resting on her chest when all of sudden Petite Princesse jumped out of the basket, clearly looking for a place to empty her bladder. We both had to act quickly; while I tried to grab the dog, Françoise jumped off the bed, tripping on the step stool, and almost falling with the baby still in her arms. We did a switch-off, with Françoise passing me the baby as she grabbed the dog and quickly ushered her out to the garden. When Françoise returned I pointed down to her pubic area to show her that she had just gone outside wearing her shirt and no underwear. It was a riot!

And just when I thought I had seen and heard everything in my line of work, there was more to come. At her last appointment, Françoise informed me that she was leaving to visit her family in France. She was devastated by the fact that she'd have to leave Petite Princesse behind. She was very concerned with the stress and anxiety her beloved puppy would have to withstand, staying at home alone all day while Françoise' husband was at work. I tried to make a joke, saying something about how most women would be happy to have their husbands sleeping with that kind of bitch while they were away. I confess that even I noticed that the little diva dog was unusually quiet. At the end of the waxing session I asked if Princesse was sick, because she looked so lethargic.

It was then that Françoise told me that since she thought the dog would "freak out" when she left, she was trying to mellow her a little bit with several different methods of dog therapy: massage, bubble bath, acupuncture...but nothing seemed to be making a difference in her mood. "Finally," she explained, "I gave Petit Princesse a Prozac pill.

"You did what?" I said in disbelief.

Seeing the horror on my face she apologized and tried for several minutes to justify the fact that she was only, well, "lightly drugging" her *chou chou* and, while she copped to the fact that this was unusual, she also said she had a checked with a veterinarian friend before doing it.

After Françoise left my office, it took me a while to regain my composure. It amazed me how far she had gone to ease her dog from a little stress. The episode reminded me of a news report on the popularity of antidepressants and the unprecedented profitability of the pharmaceutical industry. If other people start to use Françoise' approach, very soon we'll have Petzac for stressed out dogs, and maybe Petalin in case you have an over-stimulated hairy friend. Woof.

BBW Quickies

Betty's husband John had been laid off, so they decided to sit down one night to discuss their budget. The landscaper had to go; John would mow the lawn and prune the bushes himself. Betty would have to ask the kids for some help around the house, so the housekeeper would get cut, too. Their social outings as a couple would have to be minimized, and meal planning would help them control their grocery bill better.

The one thing that John would not budge on?

Betty's monthly visit to me for her BBW. He wouldn't pay Jose to do the garden, but he would definitely be paying me to groom his wife's bush!

Divine Intervention

Speaking of stress, I never had reason to keep a husband from coming with his wife to her BBW session...but that was before I met Erica and Donald. Having a friend—or better yet, your other half—in the room means more moral support and, in most cases, a more relaxed client. I can do my job faster when my client is happy and at ease. What's more, I have found that watching helps demystify the experience, especially for husbands who often think what their wives are doing is torturous. But Erica and Donald were special.

Erica is thirty-five-years old and had been a client of mine for over a year when she asked to bring her beloved with her. She works as a hairstylist, and it shows. Her hair is perfect, with long shiny golden curls. She has striking blue eyes, and a tan with an orange hue that tells me she buys it somewhere in bulk. Her slender waist and small frame only add to the attention her oversized breast implants get. There's no question she turns heads anywhere she goes, and it helps that she has a bubbly personality.

When Erica comes in alone she usually talks about her marriage. She and Donald are close in age, but he has some silver streaks peeking through his luscious dark hair. The day he came with Erica I immediately noticed how he stood, quiet and composed, speaking only when asked a question. He came across as very serious at first. When he did smile, it seemed like the sun engulfed him; he radiated. People like Donald should smile more often. I began to think of how fun it was to have a couple in together—but my joy soon left me.

Before we got started with the BBW, Erica asked me if I had time to wax her lower legs. After checking my appointment book, I said, "Sure," and got to work. A few minutes later, Donald, who was monitoring my moves, quietly and carefully asked the question, "Is that painful?"

Erica responded, "Not at all, I think I'm used to it by now and it doesn't really bother me anymore."

"Honey," he said, "I could do this for you at home. It really doesn't look that difficult to do."

Erica shot him a dirty look but in a nice voice explained that the lower legs were fairly easy to wax. "Wait till she gets to the pubic area. That definitely requires an experienced waxer's touch," she said.

Ignoring her comments, Donald went on to say that they could save the money by buying their own wax and letting him do it for her. Erica looked at him again and, without hesitation, snapped. "Do you have any idea what you just said?"

Donald just stared at her speechless. She continued, "'Do you have the faintest clue how rude you are being towards Reny's work with your stupid comment?" She was so infuriated that her eyes looked like they were going to pop out of their sockets. Her voice grew louder and louder as the scolding continued.

"My dear, dear Donald! To say something like that in front of Reny is the same as someone coming in to my salon and acting like what I do is something anybody who never attended beauty school or endured the dreaded state board exam can do. That's ridiculous! I demand that you apologize to her right this minute."

By now I was really starting to get uncomfortable with the situation, so I butted in. "Oh, please, it's okay, guys, please don't worry about it."

But Erica was exasperated and screeched again, "You jerk! Apologize to her right now!"

He ignored her and became defensive. Looking at me exasperated he explained as if she wasn't even in the room, "Reny, this is the real Erica. This woman is a psycho, a purebred bitch!"

At this point my mind started to race as I looked for a way out of the room so I could call 911 in case they started to attack each other physically. *Or should I stay and protect her from him?* I thought. *Or him from her?* I looked around the room for something I could use to fight with, just in case. When my eyes landed on the pot of hot wax, I felt a little more relaxed knowing I had my secret weapon if I ever needed it.

Erica went on huffing and puffing while I was racing to finish the most stressful wax job of my life. When Donald finally exploded, my knees began to tremble! "You bitch, wait till you see what I'm gonna do to you when we get to the car!"

Finally, I was done with the waxing—and with the two of them. I tried one last time to pacify the situation, without luck, when all of sudden Donald approached the bed and whispered into her ears seductively, "C'mon, baby, give me a smile."

Now I was completely dumbfounded, but he kept at it. "Tell me you love me, I know you do."

It took a few minutes before Erica could look straight at him and then, still flustered, muttered, "I do love you, but you haven't apologized to Reny."

He immediately apologized. At that point, though, all I wanted was for them to leave. Then the mood turned. Erica hopped off the bed, got dressed, and cheerfully wrote me a check. The next thing I knew, they were walking out hand in hand, smiling. I, on the other hand, was left shaking and dumbfounded. My heart was pounding like I had spent the morning sucking down a dozen espressos.

To this day I haven't figured out how that verbal combat escalated so fast or how they made up even faster. Perhaps it's their M.O. to have those types of feisty arguments as a prelude to some fiery lovemaking. I'll never know....

A few weeks later, Erica called to say good-bye. Donald's job had relocated him to Florida. Talk about divine intervention! I was sad to lose her as a client and acquaintance, but I felt relieved I wouldn't have to ride that emotional roller coaster again. I was also happy that, at least for now, my wax was saved from being used as a weapon.

Role Reversal

Single, hunky, Brazilian surgeon and former model seeks romantic, monogamous relationship with lovely lady. Must like picnics, candlelit dinners, cuddling by the fire, and talking. Let's take it slow.

I know, dream man, right? Believe it or not, this guy can't find a good woman. Well, he found me, but I was already taken.

Let me back up.

I met Marco in my yoga class one day. It was impossible not to notice him. He's *goooorgeous*. Tall with a well toned body, dark skin and green eyes. And his smile is to die for.

Like every healthy woman with a pulse, I'd sneak a peek from time to time during class. While the yoga instructor would be saying things like, "Pay attention to your posture... look at yourself in the mirror and concentrate in the moment...this is your chance to get in touch with your inner soul," I couldn't help but notice Marco getting furtive looks from the other women in class.

Out in the parking lot afterwards, I saw Marco in his Lexus convertible. As I approached my car, which was parked close by, he asked in Portuguese, "Is that car yours?" Surprised, I said, "Yes," and he introduced himself. His handshake was firm. And I won't lie, my heart was all aflutter. I felt like a teenager again. He had noticed my license plate with the "(heart)WAXING" " frame on it and asked me about my services. We exchanged some small talk, I handed him my card, and we went our separate ways. Little did I know at the time that Marco would become one of my most interesting clients.

The very next day I got a fairly long voicemail from him. "It was so great meeting you. I noticed and loved your energy during class (*Aaah, so it wasn't just the girls who weren't paying attention to the yoga instructor*, I thought). I enjoyed talking to you. We should get together. Will you have dinner with me? I want to see you again...." *Uh oh. Does he realize how much older I am than him? Did he not notice my wedding ring? Did I give him the wrong signal?* I ignored the message and went on about my day.

Next day, same thing: long message. "Hi, Reny. I'm sitting here listening to some Roberto Carlos and I started to think about you." Gulp. *Ignore him again*, I told myself. But all my inner devils were jumping up and down in ecstasy. FYI to all you non-Brazilians out there: Roberto Carlos is to Brazil what Julio Iglesias is to Spain. He is the most romantic singer ever. You can melt into and fall in love with just about anyone listening to his music playing in the background.

On Marco's third try he caught me off guard at the office. Again, he had date proposals. "I'm flattered," I said. "But you are twenty years late; I'm married."

He let out a long exhale, "Oh, no!"

Thankfully, my marriage is solid and my husband's a keeper. He had to be for me to decline this gorgeous man practically begging me to go out with him.

So, my hunky Brazilian suitor settled for being a client.

Soon after I started waxing his chest for him, and during each session we'd talk about our lives in Brazil. As we shared our stories, we got to know each other and our friendship blossomed. After modeling in Milan as a young man, he decided to get serious and go to university. No surprise that this narcissistic Adonis wound up in medical school and became a plastic surgeon. In spite of his fondness for the trappings of success, he has a heart of gold. He also does pro bono work on kids and adults who'd been severely disfigured in fires or accidents.

As for himself, Marco had been hurt, too—emotionally and financially—by a divorce. But his career as a plastic surgeon was really taking off. Dating? Now that was not quite as successful.

After the first few appointments, however, he started bringing girls with him. I began to feel like he was parading them in front of me for my approval.

First, there was Martha, a plain, pale girl from Boston with not much to say or offer. I tried to start a conversation while waxing her brows, but she didn't have much to contribute other than the fact that all she wanted was to move to California. Boston was too cold and she preferred our people and our warm weather. *Who doesn't?* I thought to myself.

Marco called me the very next day wanting to know what I thought of her. I rebounded with a few questions of my own. "Why are you asking me this? Do you love her?"

He said he wasn't sure but that he wanted to know my opinion. I told him I thought she might be looking for someone to take care of her in her new place of choice and that he might just be her port in a storm.

A few weeks later I got another Marco call. This time he wanted to schedule Lori, who turned out to be another nothing-to-say kind of person. No personality, but very pretty and blonde. She was a paralegal who didn't like housework.

Unfortunately for Lori, that was a deal-breaker for Marco. He can't stand a messy house.

The last candidate I heard from was Sophia. She lasted a little bit longer. A tall blonde with a perfect body, her rich parents spoiled her rotten. She'd never had to work a day in her life, and she drove a black BMW and traveled to Europe every year.

During one of her appointments she mentioned an upcoming trip to go skiing in Colorado. I told her that my husband and our boys were heading to Tahoe to do the same thing. "Oh, my style of skiing is a little different," she said. When I asked why (like I knew she wanted me to), she said, "Oh, the helicopter flies us to the top of a mountain and we ski down. It's so much more exciting." At this point, I looked at Marco for a reaction, but he was reading a magazine, oblivious to our conversation.

At another appointment she had the nerve to say that my office was smaller than her walk-in closet. But it seemed that Marco was smitten with her—at least in the beginning.

When he came solo one day, I asked about Sophia and he told me they'd broken up. You won't believe his explanation. "All she wanted was sex!" he told me.

Yes, poor Marco. He'd go out of his way to please her with romantic dinners, soft music, candles, and a crackling fire. She'd eat in a hurry and then basically molest him. One time, she jumped at him in the middle of dinner, right there on the table. "Just like in the movies," he said. Seems that all Sophia cared about was the sex.

The last straw in their relationship, however, was when Marco broke his leg and couldn't walk. He had to stay in bed with his leg in a harness, so he'd hired a home-nurse to take care of him. It bothered him that it took Sophia a week to come for a visit. When she finally called saying she was coming, he was elated. He asked his nurse to get some fresh flowers for the house and to place a chair next to his bed for Sophia so they could sit and talk and enjoy each other's company.

Well, Sophia had other plans. She came upstairs to his room, locked the door, and proceeded to undress him. I know it sounds sexy, but he looked so hurt as he was telling me this. Let me remind you, the man was in traction! From the sound of it, she basically attacked him. She jumped on the bed and started to caress his chest, rubbing her young, firm breasts on his face until she finally "forced herself" on him, he said.

As Marco continued with his story, he started to get a little angry. "There I was, defenseless and unable to move, and all that woman wanted from me was sex! In other words, Reny, she raped me. She took advantage of the situation. Don't you think?"

I just couldn't help telling him what was going through my mind. "I think maybe you overreacted, Marco," I said. "I know at least a handful of guys who would break their own legs just to have that done to them!" But Marco is not like most guys. And that was the end of Sophia.

Marco is still a client and last month he went to Brazil to learn a new plastic surgery procedure. I suggested to him that, while there, he should relax and not be too anxious to find the perfect woman.

I often think about him and all of his admirable qualities. Looks aside, he's a sweet, sincere guy who has so much to offer. But he's still alone. Perhaps it's his hotness that's working against him. Women are so eager for a taste of him, they can't see beyond the package to the real man inside.

BBW Quickies

My license plate says "(heart)WAXING."

While it is a great advertising vehicle, it can also be bothersome at times.

Once, at the supermarket parking lot, a gentleman approached me. His car was parked next to mine. He looked at my license plate and, with a devious smile on his face said to me, "Wow, love waxing. What kind of waxing do you do? Do you wax cars? Can you wax mine?"

Without missing a beat I replied, "No, I do not wax cars, sir, I wax body parts such as backs, chests, or your crotch."

Immediately, he crossed his legs and slowly got into his car muttering under his breath.

The Mushroom Cloud

A few years ago a friend of mine told me that she thought it was time to move in with her boyfriend.

"How do you know when it's the right time to take a step like that?" I asked her.

Her response? "When you fart in each other's company and it feels okay."

If that's true, then many of my clients can feel right "at home" while under my care. The passing of gas is not unusual when I've got you in some of the positions that are necessary for the BBW. I understand that it's a normal bodily function and, I assure you, after so many years in this business I consider farting part of the trade.

For the most part, it can all be blamed on food. Everyone's diet varies, and accordingly, so does their flatulence. Depending on what some of my clients ate that day, the soothing music won't be the only sound you'll hear in my waxing room. Put a days' worth of "contributions" together, and you've got a virtual symphony.

Since I have four men in my house, it is not surprising that I get my share of farts at home. In fact, I am ashamed to say that not only do my guys pass gas, they hold contests for who can do it the loudest. I've experienced times when they have a veritable chorus of farts in our family room. It truly is a feast for the senses: sight, sound...and smell.

While most women feel mortified by the thought of being caught farting, men are just the opposite. They seem to take pride in their output and could care less about those colorless, noisy, but stinky gases they pass. Their strategy is successful. When a guy farts, it's no big deal. But when a woman farts...oh, the shame! We've all had those moments when, despite our best efforts, a little toot sneaks out. For every time you've been embarrassed by an unwelcome gas bubble, there are a dozen others out there who feel your pain.

◆

Let me relay to you some stories about female clients with whom I've shared a fart or two.

Linda always schedules her BBW for the morning so she can come on her way to work. Once in a while she passes some gas and apologizes profusely, promising she won't have eggs for breakfast next time she comes in. She always tells me that she tries to hold until I'm done, but as soon as she relaxes for me to pull off the waxing strip, that captive fart finds its way out.

Anna is another chronic farter. She loves beans, and it shows—or should I say, smells? In the beginning she used to apologize every time she farted but now, after four years, farting in my company has become routine. We ignore it and just keep on talking. She told me a story about a time when she was at Macy's. She let one out in an aisle when she was by herself. As soon as she ran away from her "silent but deadly" fart, two ladies approached the same spot where she'd been. Anna said they kept staring at each other, certainly guessing it was the other one who had farted. Anna just stood there, watching and laughing quietly.

Lynn is fifty-eight years old with a pixie haircut and ultra-white teeth. In fact, she's addicted to her tooth-whitening gel. Very often she shows up with the gel tray still in her mouth and must take time to rinse before we can get started. Lynn's requests vary according to the guy she's dating. Right now she's going out with a guy eighteen years her junior, and he wants it all off. Once while I was working on her she let a quiet one escape and told me bluntly, "It must be the bean burrito I had for lunch." More gaseous emissions followed, but we just paid no attention and continued to wax. But then, as we were almost finished, she let out a loud one. I think it's what you call a "ripper." I am not kidding, it sounded like thunder, and I jumped back. This time Lynn apologized—profusely. I just started to laugh and told her to schedule her next appointment early in the morning. Before breakfast.

As a matter of fact, I really should advise all my "noisy" clients about proper pre-waxing dietary practice. No eggs, no cauliflower or broccoli. And definitely no beans! A fart is simply a bodily function. But it can betray you, leaving room for some serious embarrassment.

Take my client Helen, for example. Helen is traditional, conservative, and extremely proper. She works hard teaching her three boys how to behave appropriately. In fact, they are currently attending etiquette school. Helen brags about the fact that they are learning everything from how to use silverware properly to how to act gentlemanly in the presence of young ladies.

Well, guess what? Even proper people fart! Helen has not only farted in my presence, she also was the source of the funniest episode in my waxing room ever. If only her boys could have been there to witness it...

As I was applying powder on Helen's bikini line to prepare the skin for waxing, she unleashed a long, melodious fart. What happened next was something I had only ever seen in magazines or movies. The force of the gas coming out of her made the powder produce a white cloud in the air. It was just like an atomic bomb—a mushroom cloud. Since little fazes me in my profession, I burst out laughing! But poor Helen was devastated. I had to rattle off every funny fart story I could think of to dispel her embarrassment, and after a while she was okay.

So, next time you get yourself ready for any occasion that will require you to do some bending or stretching, remember to consume less protein. And if someone criticizes you for farting, you can politely explain to him or her that in ancient Rome Emperor Claudius legalized farting at parties, for it was believed that holding it in could cause death. Or you can take a lesson from Anna. If you inadvertently let one escape, creating a potentially uncomfortable situation, simply act oblivious and stare at the person next to you in shock.

A Delightful Mistake

Before I start waxing anybody, I always ask one question: "Is there anything else I can wax for you while we're at it?"

This way my client is reminded of something he or she may have wanted to change or add, and I can plan our session accordingly. It wasn't until one particular session with Victoria that I truly realized the importance of clarifying a client's needs.

Victoria is one of my favorite people. She is petite, bubbly, and caring. Her marriage is solid, and she is blessed with a husband who does a wonderful job of sharing those daily routines all young families have. Even with the demands of mothering three sweet girls, she keeps herself in great shape, finding time to play tennis and swim a few mornings a week; so our waxing schedule has to revolve around her tennis games or her time in the pool.

Victoria usually gets a regular Brazilian with the Landing Strip. But one day, when I asked if there was anything else I could wax for her while we were at it, I got a different answer than I expected.

She responded, "Yep. Take it all off."

I proceeded to wax the whole area, giving her what I call a "Beyond Brazilian." As usual, we were talking and laughing. Then, all of sudden, she stopped and asked, "Reny, why does it hurt more than usual?"

"That's because we are waxing off hair that has never been removed before," I replied.

She lifted her head, looked at her poosie, and said, "Oh

my God, you're waxing the whole thing?"

I freaked, explaining, "When you said 'take it all off,' this is what I thought you meant."

"Oh shit!" she exclaimed. "I was talking about my butt cheeks, not the whole poosie." At least she was wearing a bit of a smile.

"You're absolutely right, though," she continued. "I probably would have thought the same thing. Well, I guess we just keep on going!"

"I'm so sorry," I kept apologizing. "I should have confirmed with you. Please forgive me."

Not upset at all, Victoria assuaged my embarrassment and we continued on.

When she came in for her next appointment, we just looked at each other and immediately laughed, both thinking about the previous incident. After lying down on the bed, I asked her, "And, what will I be waxing for you today, my dear?"

Her response? "The whole thing!" Surprised, and wanting to make sure I clarified, I joked "The whole butt-cheek thing or the whole poosie thing?"

She laughed out her response: "The whole poosie thing!"

"Oh, baby, really? Did your shiny new poosie bring you good luck?" I asked mischievously.

Victoria went on to explain that, when she'd gotten into her car after our last appointment, she called her husband at work and said, "You are not going to believe what Reny did to my poosie today."

"Uh-oh, did she burn you?" he asked.

"Nope," she responded. "She waxed the whole thing."

"The whole thing?" he asked.

"The whole thing," she repeated. "Reny waxed my whole poosie. I am hairless."

Her husband was in a meeting but, without hesitation, explained that he was going to find an excuse to get home A.S.A.P. He wanted to get to her before the kids came home from school. She was glowing as she explained that they had had great sex that day. And her husband kept saying it was the most honest and delightful mistake Reny could have ever made.

BBW Quickies

Sage crashed her husband's Porsche the night before she was scheduled to see me. She was so nervous to tell him about the accident but, to her surprise, he didn't make a big deal about the car.

His first question and only concern seemed to be, "How are you going to get to Reny's tomorrow?"

He promptly told her to rent a car so she wouldn't miss her appointment.

Sweet Revenge

Have you ever been wronged by someone? Ever been driven to that irrational point where—if you were really, really sure no one would ever find out—you might like to get rid of the person, dump the body somewhere, and go on with your day? What about paying them back in the same way they wronged you? An eye for an eye and a tooth for a tooth, as they say. How do you react when you feel like your husband (or partner) has been misbehaving? Don't you think he or she deserves a light punishment? But how can you retaliate against a man who is usually a good father and loving husband when he acts like a jerk? If these sorts of thoughts have crossed your mind at least once, relax. You are not alone.

I readily admit that I get mad at my darling husband— very often—for stupid reasons. Lucky for him, I just can't keep my anger inside for too long, which means I don't hold grudges. My Italian/Brazilian cocktail of a temper won't allow me to get mad without letting it out. I yell. I yell so loud that I'll bet my neighbors can hear me. I also throw things at him. Nothing too hard—a pillow, or occasionally my beautiful wedding ring. But soon afterwards, I am calm again and ready to sit down with him to talk things out over a cup of coffee or a glass of wine.

Well, that's not always the case with many of my clients, who make the scenes of *Desperate Housewives* look like a walk in the park. I know many women who, whenever they are mad at their husbands, find different ways to seek their revenge. These basically good, loving souls sure are capable of doing horrible things to their partners in order to strike back against them in the name of vengeance.

❧

Maureen can't stop bitching about her husband. "He leaves clothes on the floor and shoes in the middle of the family room, as if I was his maid," she tells me, painting a picture of a man who does nothing but sit in front of the TV watching sports while she runs around like a mad woman trying to get the kids in bed.

Even if this were the case, it still came as a surprise (mostly) when she told me how she gets even with said hubby. It upset my stomach, actually. She said that she has a new way of dealing with his dirty laundry in the living room. Every time her husband upsets her, she uses his toothbrush to clean the bathroom.

"Yikes!" I exclaimed.

She jumped in, "Oh, no, no, Reny. I don't use it in the toilet, only in the sink...for now."

❧

Juliette has a more hygienic, yet more costly tactic. She goes out and buys a five-hundred-dollar pair of shoes and waits anxiously for the credit card statement to arrive in the mail. She then proudly hands the mail to her husband and waits for him to check the charges on it.

When he does, she goes far away enough in the house so that she can hear his heavy footsteps coming her way, and pretends to be busy. This is, for her, a moment of glory. He typically arrives huffing and puffing from seeing the charge, and asks her, "What on earth did you buy that cost five hundred dollars?"

With a devilish look on her face but in an angelic tone, she says, "Oh, honey, I believe that was the day you made me so angry. Forgive me, sweetie. But I didn't want to take it out on you. And I just had to go somewhere to vent my frustration. I walked and walked, and suddenly I realized I was inside Nordstrom." He goes ballistic, she feels vindicated.

When I asked Mara about her vengeful moments, she happily answered my question with a big smile on her face. "I can hold a grudge for a long, long time," she said. "Months."

Whenever her husband goes out with the guys and comes home late, half drunk, she prepares him a very special coffee that next morning. He loves strong coffee, and always insists on French Roast. Well, her "morning-after blend" involves an old bag of coffee from many Christmases past—one that has been in her pantry for at least three years. He sips, makes a face, and says that the coffee is horrible.

She replies, knowingly, "Hmmm, it may just be that your taste buds aren't very good this morning because of all the alcohol you consumed last night." Her revenge is good to the last drop.

Leticia goes further than anyone. This mother of two teenage girls serves a laxative tea to her hubby whenever he pisses her off—about once a week. The next day, he spends most of his time in the bathroom, either at home or at work. When he complains to her, she always says it must have been something he ate. She seemed to enjoy the eye-for-an-eye act, and had no remorse at all. Until one day when her vendetta worked against her.

"It was our sixteenth wedding anniversary and he didn't even get me a bouquet of flowers," Leticia whined as I waxed her.

So, true to form, the next morning she served her usual "vengeful wishes tea." That same evening, to her surprise, hubby decided to take her out to dinner to celebrate. She was thrilled and forgot all about her evil potion.

Just as they were sitting down at the restaurant, however, he started to complain of stomach pains. All of a sudden, he looked at her with a disturbed look on his face and said, "Oh Jesus, I need to go to the men's room immediately."

Nearly midsentence he bolted, running towards the bathroom. A few minutes later Leticia received a call on her mobile.

"Honey, I don't know how to tell you this, but I just shat all over the bathroom. Can you please come in here and help me?"

She walked in to find him pantless, trying to clean the floor, walls and toilet. After the initial shock she realized that he wouldn't be able to leave the restaurant in that condition. She had to call one of her daughters to bring a pair of pants to the restaurant. Anniversary dinner over.

As Leticia told me this story the following week, she said that the only thing worse than cleaning up the foul mess was explaining to her daughters what had happened. She confessed that she was also starting to worry that her husband's health could be affected by the frequency with which she was serving him the laxative, and decided to surrender her dirty tactic. I was pleased. I expected Leticia to tell me that she was going to apologize to him but she said nothing of the kind. I just hope her husband won't be interested in reading my book!

Out of all the clients I surveyed for this story, I found Desi to have the subtlest way of getting back at her husband. She simply refuses to do his laundry. For as long as she's mad at him, his drawers steadily get emptier while the laundry basket fills up. Her satisfaction comes in eight easy words:

"Honey, I don't have any underwear or socks."

This is when she reminds him of the time he disagreed with her or upset her, driving the point home to him. He apologizes and, after that, she's not mad at him anymore. The funny part is that she still ends up doing all his laundry.

Finally, I learned from one of my male clients that the sweetest revenge of all is the one that happens without any plotting whatsoever. Sometimes life has a way of taking care of things all by itself and maintaining its own equilibrium between good and evil.

Bryan is an executive that travels extensively. He's thirty-two with beautiful brown hair and abs that should be featured in an underwear ad. Sweet Bryan is also what many women would call "a waste of a good man." He is gorgeous, a simply outstanding person...and gay.

For four years Bryan was in a loving relationship with his partner, Michael. One summer, with their anniversary approaching, Bryan decided to change his flight schedules in order to surprise Michael so they could celebrate one more year of a happy life together. When he opened the door of the condo they had bought together, his jaw dropped. His luggage fell to the floor and he just stood there with his legs shaking, paralyzed by the scene. There before him was his loving partner, on the couch making out with another guy. Dazed, Bryan turned around and left. He didn't return until two days later to face Michael. But it was time to decide what they were going to do next. Michael tried some sleazy excuses, but Bryan was too hurt to accept his apologies.

After a few hours, they decided that they should split all their belongings and go their separate ways. The decisions were difficult, but solvable. The real problem came when they had to decide what to do about the apartment they'd bought together. Since Michael was preparing to leave to get his Masters in Massachusetts, Bryan had the option of buying him out. Bryan did so, but his partner—in pure Michael fashion—milked every penny out of the deal before leaving. Michael was all about dollars and cents, and he never owned up to the fact that all of this was actually happening because he had cheated. Men!

As for Bryan, he was tired of and hurt by Michael's demands of an extra one percent here, an extra one-half percent there. With a bank loan in hand, he succumbed and gave his ex what he wanted. Deep down, Bryan was hurt, but he chose to focus on his belief that life would even things out eventually. And it did.

Bryan arrived home one day a year later to a letter from the building owner saying that a developer was interested in buying the building. Bryan told me that he wasn't ready to move; he loved the neighborhood. But he also admitted that it had been tough staying in the home he'd bought with his former lover—the scene of the crime. The time came for the meeting with the developer and, at the end, Bryan was flabbergasted with the amount that was offered. He could not pass it up.

The transaction went smoothly, and Bryan decided it

was a good time for personal travel. He wanted to fly to far-away skies. His work travel kept him in the States so he'd actually never gone far beyond. Therefore, the decision was simple. He put his belongings in storage, bought an around-the-world ticket, and got ready to go.

As he was saying good-bye to friends and family, he received a phone call from Michael. It had been seven months since they had spoken. Michael had called before, but Bryan had never answered. This time, however, he remembered his faith in life's natural equilibrium, so he answered the phone. "Yes, Michael, it would be lovely to get together," he heard himself say.

They met at a café and, after exchanging a few pleasantries, Bryan told Michael about his yearlong trip around the world. With a sarcastic smile on his face Michael scoffed, "Oh? Where did you get the money for that? Did you win the lottery?"

Knowing this was that moment, that sweet moment that no dollar can buy, Bryan sipped his latte, looked into Michael's once-beautiful eyes, and replied, "Well, sort of. I just sold our old place for nine times what we bought it for."

Michael was speechless. And for Bryan, life had once again evened the score.

Since then, Bryan has continued to travel extensively all around the globe. Once in a while I get a postcard in the mail telling me what he's up to. He often says a word of gratitude for my being a good listener while he was going through that horrible phase in his life. On one of his stops in South America he met a wonderful Argentinean guy and set up residence there. In his last e-mail, knowing how much I love to dance and to eat, he told me about the tango bars and about the "unreal" barbeque. He also told me the best times to visit and that there is a guest room in his house with my name on it. I am really considering his offer. After all, despite all the bumps in the road, and all the bad people we can meet along the way, life does take care of itself.

A Small Ship in the Night

In my business, I see a lot of private parts. Yes, ladies, penises, too. They come in all shapes and sizes, let me tell you. Still just when I thought I had seen it all, I met George. When he walked into my studio, I felt like an elf. George is 6'5" and very imposing. But he's a gentle giant, like Willy in *Jack and the Beanstalk*.

George had scheduled himself for a BBW and, after the usual formalities of introductions and paperwork, I invited him to undress and lie down. His legs extended way beyond the waxing bed, which meant I'd have to maneuver around them every time I needed to get to the wax. But, hey, I'm flexible. Now, at this juncture in the session I typically start to talk to take away attention from the fact that my clients are buck-naked. I try to break the ice by asking questions, commenting about the weather or sports, anything to try and get their minds off the procedure—and also to distract them from the initial shock of when I pull off that first strip. The only difference on this occasion was that George should've been the one doing the talking in order to get me over the surprise at seeing the size of his member!

You see, George may be an XL but his, er, unit is an XXS! During the entire procedure, even though my mind was racing, I succeeded at keeping my composure. *Maybe it's because he's so tall?* I thought. *His massive frame dwarfs it.* But, no, it was right there next to my hand and I know I've seen bigger—much bigger. I must've hidden my screaming thoughts well, because he was very happy with the results and even scheduled another appointment. Still, the theory about height or foot-size being an indicator of the size of other things. Not always so, dear readers. Not always so.

I also realized that day that George is part of a new wave of men hitting up estheticians around the country to have their pubic areas waxed. These guys are realizing that a clean pubic area makes the penis look bigger than usual. Still, in George's case I couldn't see how it would help him. Instead, this experience took me back to that age-old question—does size really matter?

During my next few visits with George I learned that he is a happily married man and has two kids. As a birthday present, he gave his wife a gift certificate to my shop, and I met Maureen. George came along, and the two of them— regardless of having been married for eight years—were as affectionate as newlyweds.

After they left, I remembered a conversation with my friend Sonja whose wisdom very much applies in this case. It's not the size of the ship, but the motion of the ocean that really matters.

Blame It On Reny

If you're in the business of beautifying privates, you should expect to get teased about subsequent pregnancies, and yes, I love it! So many clients report that their BBW makes sex more frequent, foreplay more lengthy, and the whole experience more relaxing, that I have to wonder if they're on to something. And it seems that my "group clients" get pregnant in clusters, too – why is that? One particular cluster of pregnant clients was a group of friends who were all teachers at the same school. During one calendar year, four of them had newborns or were pregnant. They were unanimous in their affirmation to "Blame it on Reny". Even more surprising are the number of pregnant clients who continue waxing through all three trimesters. I tease them that they just want to impress the maternity staff.

I think Monica was determined to win the Best Looking Poosie in the maternity ward for her two pregnancies. But despite keeping her waxing appointments up to the ninth month both times, life has a way of disrupting such plans. You see, Mother Nature seems to have given her a greased birth canal. Three years ago, Monica delivered her baby in the hospital elevator. Mortified, she kept apologizing to the hospital staff for the mess. One of the nurses gently told her not to worry. Women have been giving birth in all kinds of places since the beginning of time. Going further, she added, "I remember a few years ago this woman gave birth to her baby boy right on the grass in front of this hospital!" Monica, nearly dying of embarrassment now, said "I know, I know. That was me!!"

Hail to the Chief
Times when G.W. actually helps.

Rising to the Occasion

While a hairy back and chest may be a sign of virility, sexiness, and machismo in some Latin American countries, here in the U.S. it is just the opposite. Men are shaving more than just their faces. They are trying over-the counter depilatories, they're going for laser treatments, and some are even getting burned while attempting to wax themselves. My male clientele is growing steadily. And, let me tell you, with each client there have been new experiences.

Sam arrived one morning, shaky from nerves, with a pale face and hands. His wife was one of my regular customers—and a dear friend—but this was Sam's first time. He wasn't quite comfortable with the idea of someone applying hot wax to his genitals and then ripping off the hair. Really, can't imagine why. Yes, the thought does make most men cross their legs in fear. But more and more men are overcoming the anxiety and getting Brazilian bikini waxes.

"Please come in," I said when Sam came to my door. As he started to fill out the paperwork for first-timers, I tried to distract him and make him feel more comfortable.

"It'll be a sad day for us, eh?" I said with a shrug. The 2004 election was only a few weeks away, and we're both Democrats. "Four more years of George W."

I knew this would jerk him out of his fear. I'd learned from his wife that he was a political junkie and the mention of George W. Bush was guaranteed to put some color into his cheeks.

"God, I can't even stand to look at his face, much less

think of his politics," Sam said, the stroke of his pen getting firmer and stronger on the paper as he continued. "I can't believe some of the things he's said during this campaign. I don't know if he's just an idiot or if he actually thinks he's making sense."

I nodded as he spoke, glad he was getting more animated. But when we finished and we turned to the door of the treatment room, the color once again drained from his face, which told me that Sam's thought had returned to his beloved penis and balls—and the torture he thought I was about to inflict.

"I'm sure you will be very happy with the results, and so will your wife," I said as I escorted him into the room. Sam mumbled something and smiled faintly.

"Just relax, it will be fine," I continued as I motioned for him to take off his clothes. I kept on talking, hoping to keep him focused. "I'll apply powder to your skin and spread on the warm wax in small sections, very small, and these strips of muslin will remove your hair. It will hurt, yes, but it will feel so smooth and wonderful when we're done."

"Well, Deirdre always loves it when she gets waxed," he said, and then chuckled, "I kind of like it when she gets one, too."

He laid back and I went to work. He tensed at first as I applied the wax, sure I was going to cause him incredible agony. I smoothed it, waited a few seconds, and then pulled it off, quickly rubbing the now naked area to soothe it. The first few strips are always the most uncomfortable. Soon, though, he got used to the pulling and tugging and relaxed. Every few minutes I would ask if he was doing okay, and he would nod in affirmation. He eventually seemed to get comfortable with the pattern of what I was doing.

A bit too comfortable.

Now, I always make sure to tell first-timers that, yes, there is some pain involved in the process. By the second or third time, no one seems to care much. And I just love the fact that many men find that the process is more enjoyable than they thought, but sometimes the evidence of that stands right up during the procedure!

Slowly, as I continued to apply the hot wax and pull off the strips, Sam's penis started rising to the occasion. He flushed, mortified, and started to apologize. He also tensed up, which makes doing the wax more difficult.

Calmly, I reached for his hand and placed it on his penis, pushing both a bit to the side.

"Here, hold it over here so I can finish my job," I said, trying to convey to him that this was nothing unusual during a wax on a man. By getting him a little more involved, I hoped to deflate his excitement a bit. I kept talking, using his hand to move things this way and that. But still the erection stayed. Finally, wracking my brain, I came up with the answer.

"Okay, Sam, why don't you picture George Bush's face? Better yet, think of his laugh. And those ears of his."

Sam laughed with a snort and in seconds the problem had shrunk to manageable proportions. I continued my work and was just nearing the end when Sam's penis started to rise once again. But he knew what to do.

"Sorry, Reny. Let me focus on Bush's face and the sound of his laugh."

Success again—and we were done.

Sam climbed off the table and looked at himself, a smile on his face as he turned back and forth. He dressed quickly and came out of the room to say good-bye and give me a hug. He apologized again and I thought that—whatever the outcome of the election—at least Bush's face was useful for something.

❧

It took a different kind of scare tactic to bring Joshua's flagpole down to half-staff.

Joshua is an extremely handsome man in his late thirties, wealthy and used to taking care of himself. He'd spent years getting rid of his body hair in various ways: shaving, depilatories, even trying to wax himself. When he heard from his wife that I waxed men, he immediately called for an appointment.

Joshua arrived with a Starbuck's in hand one sunny April morning, and we quickly went to work. From the beginning, he seemed to enjoy the process. First he took off his shirt and I waxed his chest. He started moaning a bit, a natural reaction, particularly during the first waxing. When I finished, he rubbed his hands up and down his chest, smiling at the smoothness of his skin, which is what most people do. It's so different from the prickly feeling after shaving. Pleased, he dropped his shorts and pointed out the area he wanted waxed on his genitals. Again, as I applied the powder and spread the wax Joshua started to moan. Maybe it was the warm room or the quiet music or the sweet vanilla smells from the lit candles. I'm not sure, but as he lay back he would groan and then there'd be a breathless gasp after every tug. Soon, his penis started to rise.

Joshua didn't apologize. He didn't even seem to notice. I continued to work with no signs of deflation.

"Are you all right, Joshua?" I asked.

"Yes," he mumbled weakly.

I applied hot wax to his sensitive skin, waited, and pulled. He moaned. Finally, I was almost finished and his penis still pointed to the ceiling. I needed to get the situation in hand. (No, not my hand!)

"Joshua," I said firmly. 'You doing okay, Joshua?' He opened his slightly unfocused eyes, his jaw slack with a burble of saliva at the corner of his mouth.

"Yes," he said, a bit confused.

"So, have you filed your taxes yet?"

"What?"

"Have you filed your taxes yet?"

He opened his eyes more widely and then creased them, wondering why I'd asked such a question at this time. But he answered it.

"No, I haven't, but I'm almost done with them." And as he spoke, slowly, his penis sunk down to his stomach. The fact that he'd had an erection almost the entire time seemed to finally sink in, and he started to apologize.

"Oh, don't worry, it happens all the time," I said. He scheduled his next appointment and walked out, happy and hairless. He's returned quite often and is now almost hair free. Still, he always teases me about the "rude awakening" I had to use on him during his first visit—and how well it worked.

I guess when it comes to giving some men Brazilian bikini waxes, there's nothing more certain than Bush and taxes.

❧

With some men, however, how high they rise is measured in money, prestige, and power. Take Bradley, for example. He's a straight, well-groomed and well-read San Francisco attorney who comes to see me once a month to keep his back and privates free of hair. He is a surfer type with a near perfect physique: tanned body, blond hair, and bright blue eyes. His address book is filled with women from all over the world and it's not hard to see why. He has good taste in cars, clothes, restaurants, and I'm sure the same goes for women.

During one visit, Bradley told me about an exotic vacation in Costa Rica where he'd gone for his scuba diving certification. During one of his practice dives, he said, he and his girlfriend were suddenly surround by two great white sharks. They circled them, coming closer and closer.

"It was a horrendous feeling, Reny. I couldn't do anything but watch the sharks as they approached," he recalled. "It was incredible. There you are, defenseless, just waiting for the attack. I just held my girlfriend and put her behind me, not knowing what to do next.

"After a few minutes, which seemed like an eternity, one of the sharks started picking up speed, swimming toward us. Just as it reached me, it suddenly turned and took off. We couldn't believe it." They swam back to the boat as fast as they could, continuously looking over their shoulders. He still doesn't know what happened. Of course, when he told me the next story during another visit, I easily understood why the shark had left him alone.

Bradley had represented a thirty-five-year-old man who had been hit by a car driven by a senior who'd suffered a heart attack on the freeway and died at the scene. "They guy broke a few ribs and one leg, and had a concussion and a few minor injuries," Bradley said. "He spent a month in the hospital. We got him $245,000 for his pain and suffering."

Bradley got his thirty-three, and the case was almost

closed when he decided to remind his client that while the man's insurance company had paid, he could get a lot more money if he went after the old man's family. "He actually got mad at me, saying that despite all the pain he went through, he was happy with the settlement and didn't want to pursue anything else. 'They already suffered enough with the loss of their father, husband and grandfather,' he said. 'It was an accident and I'm okay with what I've gotten.' Can you believe it?"

Bradley couldn't hide is discontent with the decision and went on and on as I kept waxing him. I couldn't believe how far some people would go to cash in on other people's pain. I couldn't help but remember the joke about why sharks never eat lawyers—professional courtesy. Seems to me, Bradley should be safe whenever he dives.

**YYYAAAABBBBAAAAA-DABA-
DDDDDDOOOOOOO**

Some Like It Hairy

Unwanted hair is an annoying dilemma for women and increasingly for men all over the world. One could even consider it a health and social epidemic. While some see it as a cosmetic issue, for many it can turn into a matter of low self-esteem or even depression.

The art of hair removal has been practiced for centuries, in many cultures. Even though methods vary, the razor has always been the weapon of choice when trying to get rid of hair.

Razors are incredibly accessible, and relatively inexpensive, making shaving a highly convenient habit. It can be done in the privacy of your own bathroom, and best of all it's fast and painless. You need to be cautious about the hard-to-reach areas, though, even if you have paid over a one hundred dollars for one of those state-of-the-art razors that may not have been tested by the Gillette people.

On the other hand, shaving stimulates the hair follicle, which speeds up the re-growth process. This means the hair grows back not only faster but also thicker and coarser than before. Shaving only removes the hair at the surface of the skin, and stubble can often be felt in only a few hours.

Shaving will also cause skin irritation. The appearance of ingrown hairs and double hairs is not uncommon. What can be a real nuisance is if you shave just before a trip to the beach, where salty water can sting those just-shaved areas. Ouch!

Waxing is almost the opposite of all of that. I define

waxing as "a brief and momentarily painful process with a very happy and smooth ending." It removes the entire hair from the hair follicle, which is why it's a fairly long-lasting method of hair removal. It does not irritate the skin and nerve endings like shaving does. Even better, the hair comes back softer, finer, and suppler. Eventually clear spots will be noticeable in the waxed areas. If waxed regularly, skin will remain smooth until the next hair cycle starts, which is in about two weeks—give or take—depending on background, age, sex, health conditions, and areas to be waxed.

Just like shaving, waxing can also be done at home, again depending on the area you want waxed. However, take it from me, it can be a frustrating mission and a fairly masochistic way to save a little money. Besides, burning yourself with hot wax and other waxing faux pas—like making your skin bleed—can leave your bathroom looking like a crime scene. It's very intimidating to pull a waxing strip quickly off your own thigh, and the pain can be excruciating if you do it wrong. Not to mention the gymnastic positions that are necessary to reach some areas. On the other hand, if you are a contortionist or a *Cirque du Soleil* performer, go for it!

Better yet, invest in your peace of mind and let a professional who knows how to use the wax properly do the work for you. If you leave it up to us, the ladies in the white coats, you will see that waxing is not nearly as painful as it sounds. Yes, you need to make an appointment and yes, you need to take time out from your schedule to attend your waxing session, and, yes, you have to swallow some of your modesty. But best of all, YES, you will love the results!

However, believe it or not, not everyone embraces the aesthetic of a smooth, clean pubic area. And I'm okay with that, to each his (or her) own. But it's always very satisfying for me when people decide to "go for it."

Recently my long-time friend, Marta, came for her first BBW. She even brought two friends. Seeing as how this was their big debut with this procedure, I went out of my way to explain everything and tried my best to make them feel at ease.

The trio intended to surprise their husbands, and they couldn't contain themselves. They were laughing and giggling like teenagers the whole time. This is normal; whenever my clients come as a group, laughter is sure to be plentiful. But that's not the only thing shared in the waxing room. By the end of a session, it seems like everyone's sex life becomes an open book.

Katie told us that her husband, an engineer, is a very methodical man who plans everything in their lives, always considering the smallest details. He's also relatively introverted and conservative as far as their sex life goes, and that's what Katie was trying to change with her brave decision to go for the Brazilian.

"He and I need something new," she remarked. "Something to make my man go wild. I'd love to see his wild side. If not in our daily activities, at least in our nightly ones."

Helen and her husband both work for the same pharmaceutical company, so the fact that they spend twenty-four hours a day together makes an outing with girlfriends a very special event. When she heard that Marta and Katie were coming for their waxing, she'd agreed to join them even before she learned that they would be going for something that Helen had only read about in magazines.

But Helen was adventurous and she joined the "daring" without much hesitation. In the end, she was delighted with her silky poosie and told us she was hopeful that her often tired husband would "wake up" so she would get some sex, something she had been longing for lately.

Marta's hair was the heaviest of the three girlfriends that day. I should have guessed, judging from the abundance of hair on her head. That's usually a good indicator of what lies beneath. Jokingly, I told her that she had the shaggiest poosie of my career. As a matter of fact, I could easily have easily made an Afro-Barbie doll wig with all the hair from her poosie. (As you have probably gathered I could start a Barbie shop.) "Do a good clean-up," she said determinedly. "Legs, too."

I am by no means complaining. As a matter of fact, I'd rather wax a bushy poosie than one with sparse hair. Waxing is like cleaning house: the dirtier the house is when you start, the more your cleaning job will show and the more your efforts will be noticed. If the house is almost clean when you start, the difference isn't quite as gratifying, if you know what I mean.

So, all three women left happy (and squeaky clean) that day. But two days later, I got a call from Marta saying that her husband Carlos was very disappointed. She had no idea until now: he loved the mass of hair on her poosie. "The curls," he said, "the curls were so cute."

He said it gave her poosie this unique charm that he adored and that she really should have consulted him before undertaking such a barbaric endeavor. For the next few days she was very upset with his demeanor. He was barely talking to her and was distancing himself from her in bed as if she might infect him with some mysterious disease. She told me that she even bought some new lingerie and presented herself to him one night. But he just looked at her, shook his head, and left the bedroom. Marta and her sleek poosie were left there, alone and horny.

After a bit, Carlos apologized for acting so immature, saying he knew that her hair would grow back eventually—but not before making her promise not to wax again. Poor Marta, who had been so excited with her new look, agreed to his request.

During our phone call, she started to joke about cavemen and what gruesome prehistoric creatures they were. "There very well may be a connection," I replied "and perhaps your husband is the missing link!"

So, I am sorry I won't be seeing Marta for waxing, but I will always have this picture of Carlos as Fred Flintstone, dragging Marta to bed by her hair.

Going Green

If you are considering getting waxed, relax
and go for it knowing that you may be
saving the planet.

Yes, waxing saves water since there's no need
to shave in the shower. You also won't be
contributing to the outstanding number of
disposable razors (two billion) dumped
every year in landfills.

Sticky Bottom

In any field, whenever you think you know everything, a new challenge emerges to take you back to the reality that you never stop learning!

In my first year as a licensed waxer, I came across one of these "learning moments". Vanessa, a tall 26-year-old with ample hips, came to see me after her sister confided that she was a BBW client of mine. But Vanessa wanted something more than just the BBW. She asked me if I could wax her buttocks all the way. Since I'm not squeamish, I thought *piece of cake, I just need to act like I do this all the time and figure out a good position for her to get into.*

After we finished with her BBW, I told Vanessa to lay down on her side and hold one side of her buttock while I applied wax on the other side. As I spread the wax on, I told her not to let her side go. As soon as I said that, she shifted to look at me and her hand slipped, letting her buttock down. Her cheeks immediately began to stick together. I panicked a little as she asked, "What do we do now?" I admitted that I had no idea! Then, with her buttocks gluing together, and her afraid to move, the absurdity of the situation overcame us and at the same time we burst into hysterics. Through my laughter and tears, I forcefully separated her buttocks and started to apply wax remover to the whole area. She then pulled her side up as I pulled the other side down. To our relief, both sides separated and I was able to remove all the wax. Needless to say, I learned never to wax bottoms in a position where gravity could "work against us". Vanessa and

I still laugh about the time we thought she'd have to visit the ER with a story that would make the hospital rounds for a long time!

Bonding Over the BBW

Some of the funniest moments in my waxing room have come when groups of women ventured in for a "gang waxing". As we all know, word-of-mouth is the most powerful advertising in the world. It can make or break a business. But it takes on a whole new meaning when someone like Monique, who has a group of close and open-minded friends, gets her first BBW. And the younger groups are always ready to amaze us "boomer chicks" with the latest piercing trends. Friends seem to bond even tighter when they get away from their husbands and kids and jobs for a couple of hours to get waxed and share a good laugh!

"I'll show you mine if you show me yours."

I waxed Monique for the first time after a referral from her cousin. When calling for her second appointment, she wanted me the schedule her five friends. (Yessss!!!). Over time, those friends brought other small groups, and today I'm pleased to have no less than fifteen regular clients from Benicia, California. Many live in the same neighborhood, play bunko at each other's houses, watch each other's kids, share secrets, and go on vacation together.

"Hello, Reny, hello," Monique called out one time as she marched into the waiting room, purse in one hand, bottle of red wine in the other. The group quickly followed her in, chattering and carrying cheese and crackers. They clustered in the waiting room, eating and drinking while taking turns getting waxed. I'd simply call one in after the other like an assembly line. Each had her waxing done in private, but when the last one was done, they gathered in the waxing room, undressed and compared results.

"Yours looks so cute."

"Wow, look at hers, it's beautiful."

This definitely NOT your grandmother's neighborhood coffee klatch.

"Sisterly Love."

While Monique and her gang share everything except seeing each other get waxed, Dina and Alice aren't so shy. These sisters drive more than 35 miles every month for their appointment and often bring friends along to go out with after the waxing.

During one appointment, as I had Alice's leg up and was working on her, Dina grabbed her cell phone and took a picture of Alice in all of her compromised glory.

"Hey," Alice said as she twisted around the look at Dina. Dina backed away with the phone in her hand, giggling. Their friends started to tease Alice about posting her picture on the Internet.

"Dina, you should erase that."

"No, it's funny."

"That's not funny, it's embarrassing."

"Em-BARE-ASS-ing, that's for sure."

Finally, Alice resorted to good old sibling blackmail.

"If you don't erase that picture, I'll tell Mom and Dad you're getting the 'beyond Brazilian' done and not just your legs," she said pointedly to her younger sister. Dina quickly erased the picture. Alice triumphantly held out her hand and Dina gave her the phone.

"Obstacle Course."

When late teens come in for group waxes, the conversation rolls the clock back for me more years than I care to admit. But some things never change. Teens of every generation need to chase their sense of belonging and go through periods of being as outrageous as possible. This is critical as they become independent and learn to get comfortable with themselves before they emerge as adults. My biggest group comes in five or six strong, staying in the room and talking as each takes her turn on the waxing bed. They keep me updated on the latest fashion trends, what's going on in their schools, and their dating escapades.

Once, as I started to wax Lisa, the oldest in the group, I saw that she had had a piercing just above the clitoris. I asked her why and she said: "Oh, I just wanted to experiment for a while." Such ornaments make my job more difficult since I have to be extra careful applying and removing the wax without damaging the skin in that area.

At her next visit, she told me that she was considering adding a second piercing in her poosie. I had heard enough and replied: "If you do that, I won't wax you anymore. I'm good, but this obstacle course you are creating for me is difficult to wax around." To this day I am happy to report that she hasn't added any more "hardware" down there.

"Too much of a good thing...."

Speaking of hardware, Celia's apparently hit the right spot.

Celia, Sammy and Kelly are all in college now, and they have been getting waxed together since high school. Of the three girls, Celia was always the outrageous one. Her purple hair contrasts well with her pale Irish skin. She has several piercings above her neck but after your initial surprise, you look beyond them.

One time, Celia was unable to make the group appointment. While waxing Kelly, I asked the girls how things were with Celia.

"She had her clitoris pierced," Kelly said.

"She did what?" I asked, shocked. *What in heavens are these young girls up to nowadays*, I thought to myself.

"Oh, yeah," Sammy piped in. "She says she has orgasms all day with it, just from sitting and moving around. She has orgasms while walking in the street or in the library rubbing her thighs together".

"By the time she hooks up with her boyfriend, she's so exhausted from having fun by herself that she doesn't want to have sex. Yesterday he told her if she didn't get the ring removed, he'd leave her."

Talk about too much of a good thing...

The Girl from Ipanema

Finally, I could not finish the book without sharing a very important piece of the Brazilian culture that has shaped and inspired me.

Tall and tan and young and lovely
The girl from Ipanema goes walking
And when she passes, each one she passes goes – ahhhh...

Very often during the BBW procedure, instead of some soothing music, I play samba and bossa nova, and whenever *The Girl from Ipanema* song comes up, the mature clientele reminisces about it, while the young often comment on the beauty of the song. I take pleasure telling them about this very important piece of my Brazilian culture.

I grew up singing this sophisticated song, which with the sound of samba, also universalized Brazilian music and gave birth to the "bossa nova". We Brazilians consider *The Girl from Ipanema* with its seductive and smooth sound to be the "informal" Brazilian national anthem.

It all started in 1962 when Heloisa Pinheiro (Helo as she is popularly known) call the attention of the song's composers Antonio Carlos Jobim and Vinicius de Moraes among many others just by passing on her way to the beach by the bar where they gathered. Her sensual way of swaying her hips had the men fantasizing but she was unaware of any attention whatsoever. An elementary school teacher, Heloisa was only 18 years old and a striking beauty. She was tall and her long dark hair and emerald green eyes were a beautiful contrast to her golden-brown skin.

In 1963, Stan Getz recorded the song for the first time in the famous Getz/Gilberto collaboration in New York. Joao Gilberto and his wife Astrud were on vocals, and Getz played his tenor sax. By 1964, "The Girl from Ipanema" had been on *Billboard* magazine's most-played list for ninety-six weeks. That same year, the track received seven Grammy nominations. It won four of them, beating "I Wanna Hold Your Hand" by the Beatles for best single. Today, "GFI" is claimed to be the second most recorded song in history, topped only by "Yesterday" by the Beatles. From then on, Heloisa and Ipanema Beach were known worldwide.

Her world could have turned up side down but she didn't want to lose control of her life. She went as far as posing on the beach for some newspapers and was in some magazine covers but refused offers to appear in movies or TV shows. All she wanted was to get married and start a family. In 1966 she married her high school sweetheart Fernando Pinheiro, with Tom Jobim as best man, and they raised four children.

Today, at 63 and still married to Fernando, Helo remains tan and lovely. She is a knockout who has men gawking and women shyly staring at her with a tiny bit of jealousy, perhaps wondering if they too could be that beautiful at her age.

As I got older, myth aside, I learned how to admire this legend whose friendly disposition enchants everyone who approaches her. The "celebrity aura" doesn't prevent her from posing for pictures in the streets of Rio whenever asked or hugging and kissing people the Brazilian way (a kiss on each cheek).

She is a down to earth woman who cares about her family and treats her body with respect. Her youthful beauty may be attributed to good genes, non-stop dance classes, yoga, healthy eating, and the fact that she does not smoke or drink. These days you can still see her at Carnival, gracing the tops of samba-school floats during the parade.

I visited Rio a few years ago with my husband Jeff, and the bar where the song was written is called now *The Girl from Ipanema* with the lyrics written on the walls. The bar is still going strong and is an obligatory stop for anyone visiting Rio. It's always filled with tan bodies, laughter, beautiful people and the same powerful vibe I remember from my single days when I was living just a few blocks away. My husband loved the whole experience. It was exciting to once again be right there where so much history transpired.

Helo is to Ipanema what Pele was to soccer: a celebrity who helped elevate Brazil's name with charm, beauty and respect. I hope that some day you, too, can visit The Girl from Ipanema Bar and experience the energy and sensuality for yourself.

For me, the expression of Brazilian beauty has always signified an empowerment of the self. Our bodies and our self-image work together to reinforce one another. And together they create the image we project to the world. Just walking in the warm sands of beautiful Ipanema, happy with myself and proud of how I have chosen to live my life, is extremely satisfying. Furthermore, my confident self-image extends to the warmth and caring with which I treat those around me. Knowing that by living my life out loud I show the ultimate respect for who I am has brought about great joy into my heart. Everyday that I wax someone—a Brazilian Bikini Wax for women and men—I hope that they too will walk out of my office with this emotion, the feeling that who they are is beautiful, unique and powerful.

**For Additional Copies
On-line**

www.amazon.com

**Information
About the Author &
Book Events**

www.waxconfessions.com

Questions & Comments

info@waxconfessions.com

Testimonials
(continued)

There is no other Brazilian Bikini Waxer out there like her...no joke! Reny is the best. She is so full of life, love, and personality, and makes you feel like you are hanging out with one of your girlfriends. Going for a wax is something you look forward to instead of dread. Keep up the great work, Reny! You have such a special way of making women fall in love with their own poosies!

Kris P. - Concord, CA

I go to Reny because of her personality. With her I can just talk about everything. Whether it's just chitchat or talking about more personal things in my life such as family, friends, or in my case girlfriends or lack there-of...LOL! It is easy to be comfortable around her, and even though my time in her office is a little painful, I prefer that she be the one causing the pain and not anyone else. Luv ya, Reny.

Aaron H. - Walnut Creek, CA

Reny has a way of making you feel comfortable and relaxed even when the hair is being pulled off of your privates. She will even suffer a sore back just to tweeze those last few hairs to ensure a thorough job. I feel so bad when she strains her back and neck while looking to find any leftover hairs, but that's Reny's dedication and passion for her trade. Sex has always been great with my wife, but for me the hair always seemed to be discomfort. Thank you, Reny, and thanks for giving us the means to enjoy an unbelievable sex life.

James M. - Concord, CA

I've been going to Reny for nearly ten years and I will continue going until either my hair stops growing or she stops providing her service (both are not likely). She is the only person I've gone to that is extremely thorough in waxing and is sure to snip/wax every stubborn hair. Reny's bubbly attitude and positive energy literally distracts you from the pain. My husband and I look forward to my visits.

Stacie E. - Fairfield, CA

I never dreamed that I would be getting a Brazilian bikini wax. Well, at least a partial Brazilian bikini wax. I say partial because whenever that hot wax gets to close to places it doesn't belong, I usually have to slap Reny and say, "Hey, if there is hair where you just put wax, it must have a purpose and LEAVE IT ALONE!" Of course by that time it is to late and rip—voila! It's all gone. OUCH!

I find it amusing that I look forward to my visits to the torture table with Reny. She is one of my life's most treasured people and I love her dearly. I'd better, considering she is the only person outside of my husband and gynecologist who seem to have frequent viewings of my half-naked self! There's no "leave your underwear on and she'll just do the bikini line" in this shop. Nope, take them off and away we go!

I remember in the early days when I wasn't sure how much hair I wanted left behind (the twelve-year-old bald eagle look didn't work for me or my husband). Then it finally happened. I found a way to clearly communicate the shape and amount of hair I wanted to survive the waxing, and it's been smooth sailing ever since. I'm the one that gave Reny the "airplane" analogy. I told her, "You know, I have a big airplane so I need a decent size landing strip."

Who knew such a private and sometimes painful experience could spark a friendship that I believe will last the test of time. Reny ranks up there with the "Vagina Monologue" gals—love your vagina and be proud of it. Thanks, Reny, for loving your job and sharing your passion with me (and my husband). You are the best!

Erin M. - San Ramon, CA

I've been going to Reny every month for the last four years because she has a way of making you feel comfortable. She was the first person (waxer) I ever opened my legs for. Before her, I was always too nervous. I remember being nervous to go to her. I went with my sister and Reny was joking with her and joking with me and made me feel so comfortable that I decided to go for it. I've been going to Reny every month, and I will continue to go to Reny every month for my monthly "thirty minutes of pain" just so I can have the end results. Thanks for the laughs, Reny.

Deanna A - Hayward, CA

Going to Reny to get my monthly wax and sexuality boost is a must for me! Reny has the utmost professionalism. She makes something that could be rather unpleasant a very fun, sexy, and relaxing experience. As a salon owner for over ten years, I have not come across anybody like her. That's why I drive to Reny's instead having it done in my own place. Reny's Brazilian bikini wax service is one in a million, and I send all my clients to her. She rocks!

Amy B. - Concord, CA

When I think about Reny, *magician* and *amazing* come to mind—not only because of her skill for making hair disappear leaving my skin silky smooth, but also because of the way she makes me feel welcome and at ease while I am being waxed.

During the whole visit we have fun conversations and laugh a lot. I usually cannot wait to see her. She has the talent of making me happy every month and my husband a much happier guy.

We love you, Reny!

Emily L. - Lafayette, CA

A gift certificate is where it all began. When I called to schedule a bikini wax I had no idea what I was getting myself, and my girlfriends into. When I told Reny I wanted a bikini wax she replied, "Brazilian, babe?" I said, "No, no, maybe next time," and that was it.

Five weeks passed and I was back. I could have gone to my usual salon, but I didn't. Reny was so professional, casual, and fun. When I got there she asked again, "Brazilian, babe?" And I said, "Yes! Do it before I change my mind." When it was over I was so excited about the whole experience that I told all the girls at work about it. In the bathroom later on I even showed them my very first BBW. They were all excited but a little skeptical about going in. I assured them that Reny would make them feel relaxed. "She makes you feel better than any MD I have seen. I feel I've known her forever," I said.

I mentioned to them what Reny told me in her Brazilian accent: "Oh, dahling don't be embarrassed, I see close to one hundred poosies a week and yours is no different." Today, Reny sees all of them, as well as their friends.

Monica B. - Danville, CA

I was first sent to Reny as a nervous eighteen-year-old by a mutual friend to have "something done" about my bushy brows. Not five months later, she'd convinced me to make my senior trip to Florida all the better by introducing me to the world of Brazilians. Seven years have gone by, and I'm happy to say my bikini line is still in the very capable hands of Reny. I look forward to my monthly meetings with her and the hot wax—not only for the beautification but for the ego boosts, laughs, and that motherly care and concern about my life, relationships, and family that Reny manages to impart even when inflicting serious pain on my crotch.

Reny knows secrets about me (and my anatomy) that few other people do, but she always manages to make me feel like I've got nothing to hide from the world. Who knew that hair removal could be such a fantastically fulfilling part of my life? I'm lucky to have Reny as my esthetician and confidant, and I recommend her to any and all who want a few fewer hairs in their life. They'll be getting so much more than just a wax!

Mary T. - San Francisco, CA

Reny is a very special person. She does such a wonderful job! There are not many people who could put others at ease when performing this kind of service. Her wit and charming personality make each visit fun and enjoyable. You are so busy having great conversations and laughing that you forget about the pain. Thanks for everything you do for me, Reny!

Donna A. - Rio Vista, CA

I go to Reny because she does more than provide a service: she is a caring, genuine friend. My time with her is filled with stories and laughter. After being under her care for over six years. I am used to the word "poosie" just the way she says it. As a male I have a great love for it, too!

Brian J. - Martinez, CA

After a few horrible experiences I didn't think I could go for any more waxing. But when I heard about Reny I decided to try it one more time. What a great decision! Reny really knows how to do her job. I just lie there and tell her, "Beyond Brazilian please!" The pain is momentary but the "sexy" feeling lasts for a long time. My boyfriend goes wild when I tell him I am going for my waxing appointment because he knows how smooth I will be when I come back.

Thanks, Reny, for making sex so much fun for me and my boyfriend. We are happy to have you in our lives!

Estefania - Lafayette, CA

After a series of interesting conversations with my wife where she told me I just didn't understand how itchy things can be when you shave "down there," I decided to surprise her and try it myself. After doing that wrong, I thought I'd try waxing myself instead. As you can guess, if I can't shave myself well, the home waxing results were less than fantastic. So, I decided I'd get a professional wax done, but found that there aren't many places that accept men as clients for a Brazilian. Hmm, where to go now? After a bit of Googling, I found a location close to my office that took men as clients. I e-mailed Reny and found a time for my first Brazilian.

Without really knowing what I was getting myself into, I arrived at her salon wondering just how this would go. I was a bit nervous that the pain would be enough to make me cry out, since that's what you see in The *40-Year-Old Virgin* and waxing videos on YouTube. Thankfully I had nothing to worry about, as Reny made me comfortable immediately and is great at keeping the pain to a very tolerable level. She kept me comfortable by being funny and professional the entire time. Now my biggest issue with having a smooth look is resisting the urge to show everyone just how good of a job Reny does!

John - East Bay, CA

The thought of a complete stranger looking and touching the most private of private parts can make even the most content person tense. Not to mention hot wax ripping away strip by strip of unwanted hair from down there! EEK! Yet Reny's way of making you feel at ease is magical! Not only does her candid humor make you laugh, she settles your nerves. Reny has a genuine love for her work. She possesses a gift, which is to make ugly pussies pretty. Thank you Reny!

I wouldn't go anywhere else. God help me when you retire. My pussy will be named "Chewbacca" thereafter.

Carrie W. - Sonoma County, CA

Made in the USA